July 2013

FINANCIAL COMPANY BANKRUPTCIES

Need to Further Consider Proposals' Impact on Systemic Risk

GAO-13-622

Highlights of GAO-13-622, a report to congressional committees

GAO Highlights

FINANCIAL COMPANY BANKRUPTCIES

Need to Further Consider Proposals' Impact on Systemic Risk

Why GAO Did This Study

The Dodd-Frank Wall Street Reform and Consumer Protection Act (Dodd-Frank Act) mandates that GAO report on an ongoing basis on ways to make the Code more effective in resolving certain failed financial companies. This report examines advantages and disadvantages of certain proposals, based on those identified in GAO's first report, to revise the Code for financial company bankruptcies—specifically, proposals (1) to change the role of financial regulators in the bankruptcy process; (2) affecting funding of financial company bankruptcies; and (3) to change the safe-harbor treatment of QFCs. For this report, GAO held two expert roundtables in which participants evaluated the proposals using criteria for orderly and effective bankruptcies that GAO developed in earlier reports. The criteria are minimizing systemic risk, avoiding asset fire sales, ensuring due process, maximizing value, and limiting taxpayer liability. GAO identified these criteria by reviewing literature and interviewing government officials, industry representatives, and legal and academic experts.

What GAO Recommends

FSOC should consider the implications for U.S. financial stability of changing the role of regulators and the treatment of QFCs in financial company bankruptcies. FSOC agreed that a disorderly financial company bankruptcy could pose risks to financial stability, but stated that it would be premature for FSOC to consider proposals to change the Code. GAO reiterated that its recommendation was consistent with FSOC's statutory role and responsibilities.

View GAO-13-622. For more information, contact Alicia Puente Cackley at (202) 512-8678 or cackleya@gao.gov.

What GAO Found

Because the Bankruptcy Code (Code) does not specifically address issues of systemic risk, experts have proposed giving financial regulators a greater role in financial company bankruptcies. However, according to experts at a GAO roundtable, such proposals may have limited impact and raise certain implementation issues. For example, a proposal to require notification before bankruptcy depends on when (number of days) notification would be required and with whom (which regulators). Experts noted financial companies may not know that they will declare bankruptcy even a few days before the event and could have many regulators to notify. Experts also noted ways regulators already can compel financial companies to declare bankruptcy, and that changing the Code to allow regulators to place firms in bankruptcy involuntarily could temporarily place a firm in an uncertain legal status, eroding firms' values and endangering market stability. Other options, such as having regulatory standards forcing the firm into bankruptcy, could improve the likelihood of an orderly resolution, according to these experts. Although the proposals reflect the need to minimize systemic effects of financial company bankruptcies, the Financial Stability Oversight Council (FSOC)—charged with responding to threats to financial stability—has not considered changes to the Code. Consideration could improve FSOC's ability to address such threats in a timely and effective manner.

Experts emphasized that funding is needed to facilitate orderly and effective financial company bankruptcies. They generally agreed that prohibiting all federal funding or guarantees of private funding likely would lead to fire sales of assets. They agreed that fully secured funding should be used only to provide short-run liquidity and not for bailouts of insolvent firms' creditors. Experts suggested a private-sector fund could be created for this purpose. Such funds could be collected voluntarily, through routine assessments (before a bankruptcy), or through a facility similar to the one created for the Orderly Liquidation Authority, which allows federal funding at the time of a bankruptcy and later recovery of funds through an industry assessment. Experts noted some difficulties associated with these proposals, including determining whether a firm was insolvent or needed liquidity, and identifying permissible types of collateral.

Generally, experts did not agree on advantages or disadvantages of proposals to change the safe-harbor treatment of qualified financial contracts (QFC). The Code exempts QFCs, such as derivatives, from the automatic stay that generally prevents creditors from taking company assets in payment of debts before a case is resolved. It also exempts QFCs from provisions that allow bankruptcy judges to "avoid" contracts entered into within specified times before a filing. Proposals to change QFC treatment—subjecting all or some contracts to the automatic stay on a permanent or temporary basis and removing the avoidance exemptions—might address issues raised by extensive contract terminations in the early days of financial company bankruptcies. Experts said it was unclear what lessons should be learned from those experiences. Many noted that narrowing the exemptions would reduce the size of derivative markets, but views varied about whether such narrowing would increase or decrease systemic risk. Some experts said that the current safe harbors decrease systemic risk, while others said they increase it by making firms more dependent on less-reliable short-term financing.

_____ **United States Government Accountability Office**

Contents

Abbreviations

AOUSC	Administrative Office of the U.S. Courts
Federal Reserve	Board of Governors of the Federal Reserve System
CFTC	Commodity Futures Trading Commission
DIP	debtor-in-possession
Dodd-Frank Act	Dodd-Frank Wall Street Reform and Consumer Protection Act
FDIC	Federal Deposit Insurance Corporation
FSOC	Financial Stability Oversight Council
LBHI	Lehman Brothers Holdings, Inc.
LBI	Lehman Brothers, Inc.
NAS	National Academy of Sciences
NAIC	National Association of Insurance Commissioners
OLA	Orderly Liquidation Authority
QFC	qualified financial contract
SEC	Securities and Exchange Commission
SIPA	Securities Investor Protection Act
SIPC	Securities Investor Protection Corporation
TARP	Troubled Asset Relief Program
Code	U.S. Bankruptcy Code
Treasury	U.S. Department of the Treasury

GAO

U.S. GOVERNMENT ACCOUNTABILITY OFFICE

441 G St. N.W.
Washington, DC 20548

July 18, 2013

Congressional Committees:

The 2007-2009 financial crisis and the failures of large, complex financial companies led some experts to question the adequacy of the U. S. Bankruptcy Code (Code) for effectively reorganizing or liquidating these companies without causing further harm to the financial system.[1] Questions raised about the effectiveness of the Code have prompted some financial and legal experts—sometimes working in interdisciplinary groups—as well as government officials and members of Congress to propose changes to the Code, or to the supervisory process leading to a bankruptcy filing.

The Dodd-Frank Wall Street Reform and Consumer Protection Act (Dodd-Frank Act) mandates that we study, at first annually and then at specified intervals, issues including the effectiveness of the Code in facilitating the orderly liquidation or reorganization of financial companies and ways to make the orderly liquidation process under the Code for financial companies more effective.[2] In July 2011, we issued our first report, which addressed the mandate's requirements and included proposals for revising the Code to improve the orderliness and effectiveness of financial company bankruptcies.[3] In July 2012, we issued our second report that addressed actions taken to implement the Orderly Liquidation Authority (OLA) created by the Dodd Frank Act. OLA authorizes the Secretary of the Treasury to appoint the Federal Deposit Insurance Corporation (FDIC) as a receiver when, among other things, the failure of a financial company would have serious adverse effects on financial stability in the

---

[1] Insured depository institutions and insurance companies may not file for debtor protection under the U.S. Bankruptcy Code, and broker-dealers qualify for liquidation, but not reorganization.

[2] Dodd-Frank Wall Street Reform and Consumer Protection Act, Pub. L. No. 111-203, § 202(e), 124 Stat. 1376 (2010).

[3] See GAO, *Bankruptcy: Complex Financial Institutions and International Coordination Pose Challenges* GAO-11-707 (Washington, D.C.: July 19, 2011).

United States and taking action under OLA would avoid or mitigate such adverse effects.[4]

We focus in this report on the advantages and disadvantages of proposals from experts, government officials, and legislators to change the Code to make bankruptcies of financial companies (especially those that pose systemic risk to the financial system) more orderly and effective. Specifically, this report examines the advantages and disadvantages of proposals (1) to change the role of financial regulators and the Department of the Treasury in financial company bankruptcies; (2) affecting the funding of financial company bankruptcies, and (3) to change the safe-harbor treatment of certain financial contracts—including derivatives and repurchase agreements.[5]

To address these objectives, we reviewed our earlier work under the mandate and that of the Administrative Office of the U.S. Courts (AOUSC) and the Board of Governors of the Federal Reserve (Federal Reserve), which have similar mandates.[6] For this engagement we reviewed more recent literature to update the proposals we earlier identified for modifying the Code. We relied on criteria for orderly and effective bankruptcies that were developed during our earlier work. These criteria included minimizing systemic risk, avoiding fire sales, maximizing value, promoting due process, and limiting taxpayer liability. To evaluate the proposals relative to these criteria, we conducted two expert roundtables in which participants evaluated the proposed changes to the role of regulators and the safe-harbor treatment of certain financial contracts in financial company bankruptcies. These roundtables were conducted with the assistance of the National Academy of Sciences

---

[4]See GAO, *Bankruptcy: Agencies Continue Rulemakings for Clarifying Specific Provisions of Orderly Liquidation Authority* GAO-12-735 (Washington, D.C.: July 12, 2012).

[5]Such contracts are often referred to as qualified financial contracts because they qualify for safe harbor treatment—that is, they are not subject to the automatic stay in bankruptcy proceedings that generally stops most lawsuits, foreclosures, and many other collection activities against the debtor.

[6]See GAO-11-707; GAO-12-735; AOUSC, *Report Pursuant to Section 202(e) of the Dodd-Frank Wall Street Reform and Consumer Protection Act of 2010*, (Washington, D.C.: July 2011) and *Second Report Pursuant to Section 202(e) of the Dodd-Frank Wall Street Reform and Consumer Protection Act of 2010*, Pub. L. No. 111-203 (2010), (Washington, D.C.: July 2012); and Federal Reserve, *Study on the Resolution of Financial Companies under the Bankruptcy Code* (Washington, D.C.: July 2011).

(NAS). Roundtable participants included bankruptcy judges, practicing attorneys, financial regulators, industry representatives, and academics. We chose the roundtable participants based on their publications demonstrating an expertise in bankruptcy and financial regulation, input from regulatory bodies and industry groups, and suggestions from NAS. Roundtable participants discussed the proposals in relation to the criteria of orderliness and effectiveness, potential outcomes of implementing the proposals, and how impediments to implementing them might be overcome. During our work, we also met with officials from AOUSC, the Commodity Futures Trading Commission (CFTC), FDIC, the Board of Governors of the Federal Reserve System (Federal Reserve), Financial Stability Oversight Council (FSOC), U.S. Department of Justice, National Association of Insurance Commissioners (NAIC), Securities and Exchange Commission (SEC), and U.S. Department of the Treasury (Treasury). See appendix I for more information on our scope and methodology and appendix II for more information on the expert roundtables.

We conducted this performance audit from October 2012 to July 2013, in accordance with generally accepted government auditing standards. Those standards require that we plan and perform the audit to obtain sufficient, appropriate evidence to provide a reasonable basis for our findings and conclusions based on our audit objectives. We believe that the evidence obtained provides a reasonable basis for our findings and conclusions based on our audit objectives.

Background

Bankruptcy is a federal court procedure conducted under the Code. The goals of bankruptcy are to give individuals and businesses a "fresh start" by eliminating or restructuring debts they cannot fully repay and help creditors receive some payment in an equitable manner. The filing of a voluntary bankruptcy petition operates as an "automatic stay" that generally stops lawsuits, foreclosures, and most other collection activities against the debtor, allowing the debtor time to eliminate or restructure its debts. In bankruptcy, equitable treatment of creditors means that all creditors with substantially similar claims shall be classified similarly and receive the same treatment.[7] For example, a class of secured creditors —

---

[7]This treatment is also called *pari passu*, meaning "on equal footing," and in usage often refers to treating things equally, without showing preference. In the context of bankruptcy, it refers to creditors of the same class receiving the same prorated (or *pro rata*) share of payment, according to the amount of the claim.

those with liens or other secured claims against the debtor's property—will receive similar treatment. Secured creditors are more likely to get some debt repaid than general unsecured creditors, and creditors generally receive payment of their debts before shareholders receive any return of their equity in the failed company.

Bankruptcy Proceedings

Business debtors that are eligible for protection under the Code may qualify for liquidation, governed primarily by Chapter 7 of the Code, or reorganization, governed by Chapter 11.[8] Proceedings under both Chapters 7 and 11 can be voluntary (initiated by the debtor) or involuntary (generally initiated by at least three creditors). However, in an involuntary proceeding, the debtor can defend against the proceeding, including presenting objections within 21 days of being served the summons of the proceeding. The judge subsequently decides whether to grant the creditors' request and permit the bankruptcy to proceed, dismiss the request, or enter any other appropriate order.

A reorganization proceeding under Chapter 11 allows debtors, such as commercial enterprises, to continue some or all of their operations as a way to satisfy creditor claims. The debtor typically remains in control of its assets, and is called a debtor-in-possession (DIP). The court also, under certain circumstances, can direct the U.S. Trustee to appoint a Chapter 11 trustee to take over the affairs of the debtor.[9] As shown in figure 1, a firm going through a Chapter 11 bankruptcy generally will pass through several stages.

---

[8]A liquidation proceeding—under Chapter 7—is a court-supervised procedure by which a trustee takes over the assets of the debtor's estate, reduces them to cash, and makes distributions to creditors in accordance with the Code's priority scheme. This report discusses in depth Chapter 11 reorganization.

[9]If certain conditions are met, the court directs the U.S. Trustee to appoint a Chapter 11 trustee upon request of the U.S. Trustee, certain other parties, or on its own motion.

Figure 1: Chapter 11 Process, 2013

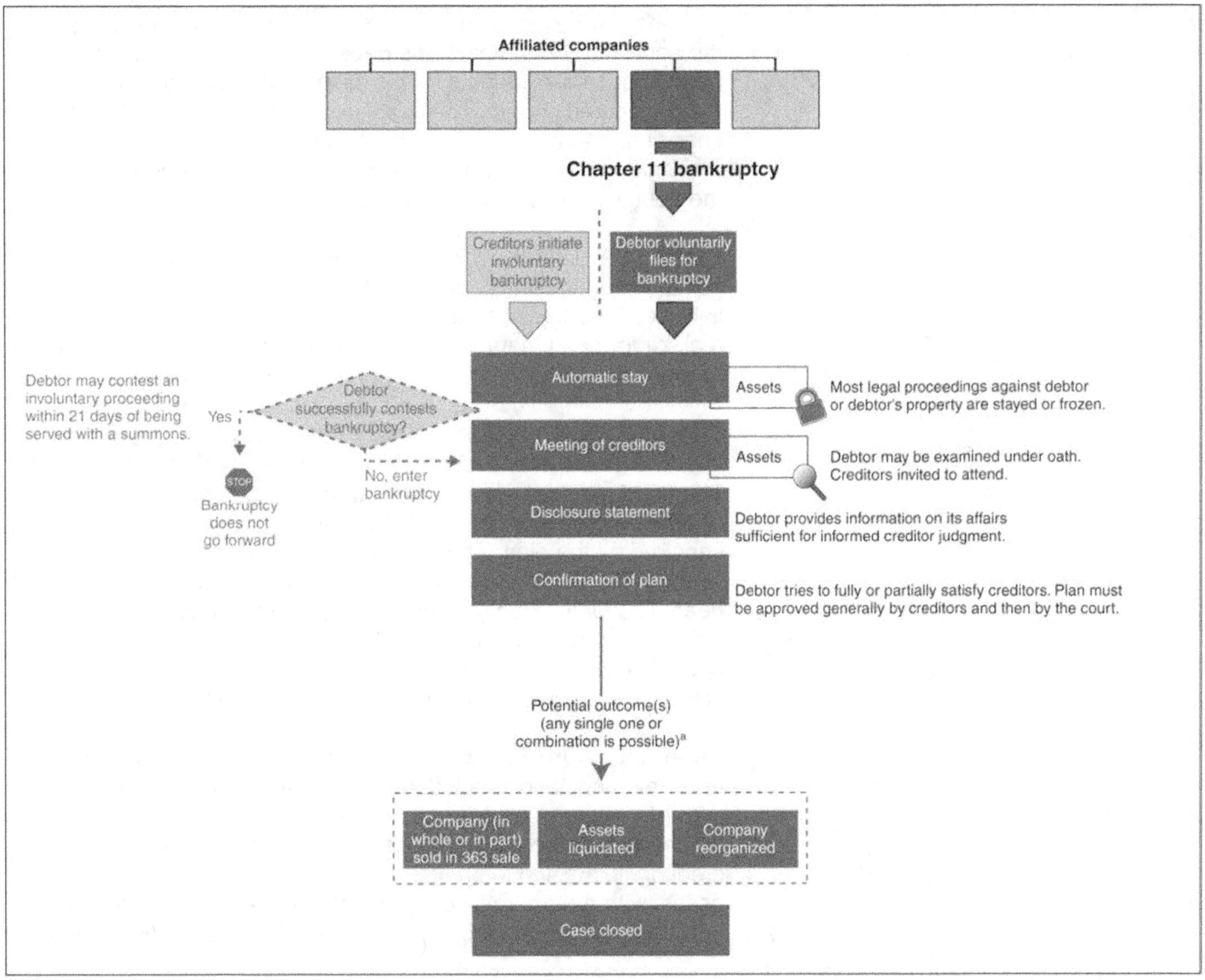

Affiliated companies

Chapter 11 bankruptcy

Creditors initiate involuntary bankruptcy

Debtor voluntarily files for bankruptcy

Debtor may contest an involuntary proceeding within 21 days of being served with a summons.

Debtor successfully contests bankruptcy?

Yes

No, enter bankruptcy

STOP
Bankruptcy does not go forward

Automatic stay — Assets — Most legal proceedings against debtor or debtor's property are stayed or frozen.

Meeting of creditors — Assets — Debtor may be examined under oath. Creditors invited to attend.

Disclosure statement — Debtor provides information on its affairs sufficient for informed creditor judgment.

Confirmation of plan — Debtor tries to fully or partially satisfy creditors. Plan must be approved generally by creditors and then by the court.

Potential outcome(s) (any single one or combination is possible)[a]

Company (in whole or in part) sold in 363 sale

Assets liquidated

Company reorganized

Case closed

Source: GAO analysis of U.S. Court information.

[a]Potential outcomes also include dismissal of the case or conversion to a Chapter 7 liquidation. A 363 sale refers to that section of the Code which applies to sales that are free and clear of creditor claims.

Each stage of the Chapter 11 process has key attributes:

First-day motions. The most common first-day motions relate to the continued operation of the debtor's business and involve matters such as requests to use cash collateral—liquid assets on which secured creditors have a lien or claim—and obtaining financing, if any. They may include a motion to pay the prebankruptcy claims of critical vendors—those deemed vital to the debtor's continued business operations.

Disclosure. The disclosure statement filed after the bankruptcy petition filing must include information on the debtor's assets, liabilities, and business affairs sufficient to enable creditors to make informed judgments about how to vote on the debtor's plan of reorganization and must be approved by the bankruptcy court.

Plan of Reorganization. A debtor has an exclusive right to file a plan of reorganization within the first 120 days of bankruptcy.[10] The court may not confirm the plan unless a sufficient proportion of allowed creditors has accepted the plan or would not be impaired by the plan. The court's approval also depends on whether there are dissenting classes of creditors. If a plan has not been filed by the debtor within 120 days or accepted by a sufficient number of creditors after 180 days, any interested party—including creditors—may file a plan. The plan divides creditors into classes, prioritizing payments to creditors.

Reorganization. Possible Chapter 11 outcomes, which can be used in combination, include (1) sale of the company (in whole or in part), which is sometimes called a section 363 sale because that section of the Code applies to sales that are free and clear of creditor claims and interests; (2) liquidation of the company's assets with the approval of the court through means other than a 363 sale; and (3) actual reorganization of the company in which it

---

[10]Also, there are many other findings a court must make in order to confirm a plan of reorganization, aside from acceptance or lack of impairment. For example, the court must find that the plan is feasible. Additionally, the 180-day rule allowing third parties to file a plan is tied to voting (i.e., acceptance of the plan by a sufficient number of impaired creditors) on a plan filed by the debtor and not just court approval. *See* Code section 1121(c)(3).

emerges from bankruptcy with new contractual rights and obligations that replace or supersede those it had before filing for bankruptcy.[11]

The debtor, creditors, trustee, or other interested parties, may initiate adversary proceedings—in effect, a lawsuit within the bankruptcy case to preserve or recover money or property to subordinate a claim of another creditor to their own claims, or for similar reasons. Furthermore, the Chapter 11 trustee or others may bring a preference action (a type of avoidance action) challenging certain payments made by a debtor to a creditor generally within 90 days prior to the bankruptcy filing.[12] In addition, fraudulent avoidance actions generally can be taken on transfers made within 2 years prior to a bankruptcy if payments are determined to be fraudulent. As such, an avoidance action can question the payment as a preferential or fraudulent transfer of assets and require payments to be returned to the debtor.

Financial Companies and the Bankruptcy Code

Large, complex financial companies that are eligible to file for bankruptcy generally file under Chapter 11 of the Code. Such companies operating in the United States engage in a broad range of financial services including commercial banking, investment banking, securities and commodities trading, derivatives transactions, and insurance. Many of them are organized under both U.S. and foreign laws. The U.S. legal structure is frequently premised upon the ownership by a parent holding company of various regulated subsidiaries (such as depository institutions, insurance companies, broker-dealers, and commodity brokers) and other nonregulated subsidiaries that engage in a variety of financial activities. Many of these businesses have centralized business lines and operations that may be housed in a holding company or in one or more subsidiaries. Smaller banking institutions also are organized as holding companies, but many of these hold few, if any, assets outside a depository institution and generally engage in a narrower range of activities.

---

[11]Potential outcomes also include dismissal of the case or conversion to a Chapter 7 liquidation.

[12]A preference action can be asserted for payments made to an insider within a year prior to the bankruptcy filing.

Certain financial institutions may not file as debtors under the Code and other entities face special restrictions in using the Code:[13]

- **Insured depository institutions.** Under the Federal Deposit Insurance Act, FDIC serves as the conservator or receiver for insured depository institutions placed into conservatorship or receivership under applicable law.[14]

- **Insurance companies.** Insurers generally are subject to oversight by state insurance commissioners, who have the authority to place them into conservatorship, rehabilitation, or receivership.

- **Broker-dealers.** Broker-dealers can be liquidated under the Securities Investor Protection Act (SIPA) or under a special subchapter of Chapter 7 of the Code. However, broker-dealers may not file for reorganization under Chapter 11.[15]

- **Commodity brokers.** Commodity brokers, also known as futures commission merchants, are restricted to using only a special subchapter of Chapter 7 for bankruptcy relief.[16]

---

[13]Financial companies that the Secretary of the Treasury determines meet the conditions specified under OLA—including that their failure and resolution under otherwise applicable federal or state law would have serious adverse effects on financial stability in the United States—may be resolved under an FDIC receivership, broadly similar to that currently used to resolve insured depositories.

[14]12 U.S.C. § 1821(c).

[15]Chapter 7 of the Code contains special provisions for the liquidation of stockbrokers. 11 U.S.C. §§ 741-753. Under SIPA, the Securities Investor Protection Corporation (SIPC) initiates a liquidation proceeding, the primary purpose of which is to protect customers against financial losses arising from the insolvency of their brokers. Once a protective decree has been applied for, any other pending bankruptcy proceeding involving the debtor stockbroker is stayed, and the court where the application is filed has exclusive jurisdiction over that stockbroker. SIPC participation can displace a Chapter 7 liquidation pending the SIPA liquidation, but provisions of the Code apply in a SIPA liquidation to the extent they are consistent with SIPA. See 15 U.S.C. §§ 78eee(b)(2)(B), 78fff(b). Because the stockbrokers discussed in this report are also dealers registered with SEC as broker-dealers, we generally use broker-dealer rather than stockbroker in this report.

[16]Chapter 7 of the Code contains special provisions for commodity broker liquidation (11 U.S.C. §§ 753, 761-767), and CFTC's rules relating to bankruptcy are set forth at 17 C.F.R. § 190.01 et seq.

Current Role of Financial Regulators in Bankruptcy Proceedings

Regulators often play a role in financial company bankruptcies. With the exception of CFTC and SEC, the Code does not explicitly name federal financial regulators as a party of interest with a right to be heard before the court. In practice, regulators frequently appear before the court in financial company bankruptcies. For example, as receiver of failed insured depository institutions, FDIC's role in bankruptcies of bank holding companies is typically limited to that of creditor. CFTC has the express right to be heard and raise any issues in a case under Chapter 7. SEC has the same rights in a case under Chapter 11. SEC may become involved in a bankruptcy particularly if there are issues related to disclosure or the issuance of new securities. SEC and CFTC also are involved in Chapter 7 bankruptcies of broker-dealers and commodity brokers. In the event of a broker-dealer liquidation, pursuant to the SIPA, the bankruptcy court retains jurisdiction over the case and a trustee, selected by the Securities Investor Protection Corporation (SIPC), typically administers the case. SEC may join any SIPA proceeding as a party.

The Code does not restrict the federal government from providing DIP financing to a firm in bankruptcy, and in certain cases it has provided such funding, as it did in the bankruptcies of General Motors and Chrysler with financing under the Troubled Asset Relief Program (TARP).[17] The authority to make new financial commitments under TARP terminated on October 3, 2010. In July 2010, the Dodd-Frank Act amended section 13(3) of the Federal Reserve Act to prohibit the establishment of an emergency lending program or facility for the purpose of assisting a single and specific company to avoid bankruptcy. Nevertheless, the Federal Reserve may design emergency lending programs or facilities for the purpose of providing liquidity to the financial system.[18]

The federal government also has provided financial support to companies who later declared bankruptcy. For example, CIT Group, Inc. received funding from TARP in 2008. CIT subsequently declared bankruptcy under Chapter 11 in 2009 and was reorganized.

---

[17]In a bankruptcy proceeding, creditors often provide financing for the debtor to have immediate cash as well as ongoing working capital during a reorganization process. This financing is called DIP financing.

[18]Dodd-Frank Act, Pub. L. No. 111-203, § 1101(a).

Current Safe-Harbor Treatment for Financial Contracts under the Code

Although the automatic stay generally preserves assets and prevents creditors from taking company assets in payment of debts before a case is resolved and assets are distributed in a systematic way, it is subject to exceptions, one of which can be particularly important in a financial institution bankruptcy. Commonly referred to as a safe harbor, this exception pertains to certain financial and derivative contracts, often referred to as qualified financial contracts (QFC).[19] The types of contracts eligible for the safe harbors are defined in the Code. They include derivative financial products, such as forward contracts and swap agreements that financial companies (and certain individuals and nonfinancial companies) use to hedge against losses from other transactions or speculate on the likelihood of future economic developments.[20] Repurchase agreements, collateralized instruments that provide short-term financing for financial companies and others, also generally receive safe-harbor treatment.

Safe-harbor treatment was first added to the Code in 1982 for forward contracts, commodity contracts, and securities contracts.[21] In a recent change, the Code's definition of repurchase agreements was expanded (in 2005) to include, among other things, agreements for the transfer of mortgage related securities, mortgage loans, interests in mortgage-related securities or mortgage loans, and government securities issued by countries that are members of the Organisation of Economic and Co-operation and Development, thereby expanding the scope of contracts subject to the safe-harbor treatment. According to the legislative history, the purpose of these safe harbors is to maintain market liquidity and

---

[19]The term "qualified financial contract" is not used in the Code.

[20]A swap is a type of derivative that involves an ongoing exchange of one or more assets, liabilities, or payments for a specified period. Financial and nonfinancial firms use swaps and other over-the-counter derivatives to hedge risk, or speculate, or for other purposes. A futures contract is a contract that is standardized and traded on an organized futures exchange, while a forward contract is privately negotiated among the buyer and seller.

[21]In general, a commodity contract is a contract between two parties where the commodities buyer agrees to purchase from the commodities seller a fixed quantity of a commodity at a fixed price on a fixed date in the future. A "forward contract" is a contract for the purchase, sale, or transfer of a commodity with a maturity date more than two days after the contract is entered into. A securities contract generally refers to a contract defining a financial agreement between counterparties. A securities contract includes contracts for the purchase and sale of various financial products such as a group or index of securities, mortgage loans, certificates of deposit, and extensions of credit for settlement purposes. See appendix III for more information on securities contracts.

reduce systemic risk, which we define as the risk that the failure of one large institution would cause other companies to fail or that a market event could broadly affect the financial system rather than just one or a few companies.

Under the safe-harbor provisions, most counterparties that entered into a qualifying transaction with the debtor may exercise certain contractual rights even if doing so would otherwise violate the automatic stay.[22] In the event of insolvency or the commencement of bankruptcy proceedings, the nondefaulting party in a contract may liquidate, terminate, or accelerate the contract, and may offset (net) any termination value, payment amount, or other transfer obligation arising under the contract when the debtor files for bankruptcy. That is, generally nondefaulting counterparties subtract what they owe the bankrupt counterparty from what that counterparty owes them (netting), often across multiple contracts. If the result is positive, the nondefaulting counterparties can sell any collateral they are holding to offset what the bankrupt entity owes them. If that does not fully settle what they are owed, they are treated as unsecured creditors in any final liquidation or reorganization.

Safe-harbor provisions also generally exempt certain payments made under financial contracts from a preference action seeking to recover any payment made by a debtor to a creditor generally within 90 days of filing for bankruptcy. In addition, they exempt fraudulent transfers made to financial contract counterparties generally within 2 years prior to a bankruptcy unless the payments are determined to have been intentionally fraudulent. Trustees cannot question the payment made in connection with these contracts as a preferential or fraudulent transfer of assets and cannot require the payments to be returned to the debtor. See appendix III for more information on the current safe-harbor treatment for derivative and repurchase agreement contracts.

---

[22]A contractual right includes a right set forth in the rules or bylaws of, among others, a derivatives clearing organization, a multilateral clearing organization, a national securities exchange or association, or a securities clearing agency.

Experts Agreed That Changing Regulatory Involvement May Have Varying Impacts and Needs Further Consideration

Experts at our roundtables evaluated proposals to change the roles of regulators in financial company bankruptcies. Specifically, they discussed proposals to require firms to notify and consult with regulators prior to a bankruptcy; allow regulators to commence an involuntary bankruptcy; provide regulators with standing or a right to be heard in bankruptcy court; and have regulators determine how subsidiaries might be consolidated in a bankruptcy. The experts noted that the proposals could have varying impacts on the bankruptcy process. For example, they viewed most of the proposals as having limited impact because regulators already have similar roles in bankruptcies, whereas efforts to consolidate subsidiaries in a bankruptcy would undermine key legal and regulatory constructs. Although experts broadly supported regulatory involvement in financial company bankruptcies, they said the proposed changes raise several implementation issues, such as determining the number of days prior to a bankruptcy that a company would be required to notify regulators and which regulator(s) to notify. As a result, the proposals require further consideration. FSOC, which is charged with identifying and responding to risks to financial stability that could arise from the failure of large financial companies, has been identified in some proposals as a regulator that should be notified.[23] However, FSOC has not yet considered implications of changes to the role of regulators in the bankruptcies of financial companies.

Proposals to Further Involve Financial Regulators in Financial Company Bankruptcies

Several proposals have been made by financial and legal experts, as well as government officials, to further involve regulators in financial company bankruptcies. The experts at our first roundtable discussed four such proposals we identified in our 2011 study.[24]

---

[23]The Dodd-Frank Act does not assign FSOC a direct role in deciding whether a company should go through OLA.

[24]We provided the experts with another proposal on granting regulators the right to file reorganization plans and motions for sale of property but experts spent almost no time addressing it so it is not included in this discussion.

Require debtors to notify and consult with regulators (primary, functional, Financial Stability Oversight Council, foreign, or other) in advance of filing for bankruptcy.[25] Bankruptcy-related proposals introduced in the 111th Congress included a notification period.[26] In prior work, we found that the notice period was intended to provide the regulator with some time to facilitate actions to minimize the systemic impact of the bankruptcy.[27] During that time, the regulator might be able to find ways to maintain critical functions, facilitate an asset sale, identify potential creditors that would provide financing for the debtor, or determine if a proceeding under OLA would be more appropriate. This extra time for preparation could help to maintain the value of the institution and reduce systemic disruptions to the wider economy.

Allow regulators to commence an involuntary bankruptcy if the firm is insolvent or in imminent danger of becoming insolvent. This proposal was included in the proposal made by the Hoover Institution resolution project group to have a separate bankruptcy chapter in the Code—Chapter 14—for large financial companies.[28] The authors of that proposed chapter noted that under the existing Code, an involuntary bankruptcy proceeding can commence when a firm generally is not paying its debts as they become due unless the debts are subject to a legitimate dispute. For large financial companies, allowing involuntary

---

[25]The Gramm-Leach-Bliley Act defines a federal functional regulator as (a) the Board of Governors of the Federal Reserve System, (b) the Office of the Comptroller of the Currency, (c) the Board of Directors of FDIC, (d) the Director of the Office of Thrift Supervision (no longer existent), (e) the National Credit Union Administration Board, and (f) the Securities and Exchange Commission.

[26]*Bankruptcy Integrity and Accountability Act*, Senate Amendment 3832, 111th Cong., 2nd sess., Congressional Record (May 5, 2010): S3620-3624 and *Consumer Protection and Regulatory Enhancement Act*. HR 3310, 111th Cong., 1st sess., *Congressional Record* (July 24, 2009): E1964-E1967.

[27]See GAO-11-707.

[28]The Hoover Institution resolution project group was established in 2009 under the auspices of the Working Group on Economic Policy at the Hoover Institution at Stanford University. The group has proposed that a new chapter—Chapter 14—of the Code be created to address bankruptcies of large financial companies. For these proposals see Kenneth E. Scott and Thomas Jackson, eds., *Bankruptcy Not Bailout: A Special Chapter 14* (Stanford, Calif.: Hoover Institution Press, 2012).

bankruptcies in response to balance sheet insolvency may allow regulators to initiate a bankruptcy at a time when they could still limit the spread of damage to other financial companies. The Chapter 14 proposal specifically provides primary regulators power to commence an involuntary case against a financial company in the event that the firm's assets are less than its liabilities, at fair valuation, or the firm has unreasonably small capital.

Allow regulators of the debtor or its subsidiaries to have standing or a right to be heard in the courts to raise issues relative to regulation. Proposals introduced in the 111th Congress contained a provision to allow certain financial regulators the right to be heard during a bankruptcy case.[29] The proposals granted the functional regulator, Financial Stability Oversight Council, Federal Reserve, Treasury, and any agency charged with administering a nonbankruptcy insolvency regime for any component of the debtor the right to be heard on any issue in a bankruptcy case.[30] Experts have contended that regulated institutions have more complicated legal structures and products than others; thus, having regulatory expertise would provide more timely information to the judge and could lead to resolutions that better preserve asset value.[31]

Consider the role of regulators in determining what subsidiaries should be included in a bankruptcy proceeding and the extent to which complex firms might be consolidated in bankruptcy. This proposal would give regulators a role in determining whether the court should consider the filing of a financial company as a whole under processes similar to the doctrine of substantive consolidation—a rarely used procedure. In substantive consolidation, the intercompany liabilities of related companies are eliminated, the assets of these companies are pooled, and the companies' liabilities to third parties are paid from

---

[29]See *Bankruptcy Integrity and Accountability Act* Senate Amendment 3832, and *Consumer Protection and Regulatory Enhancement Act.* HR 3310.

[30]The House proposal included an entity with a similar conceptual function to FSOC, which it called the Market Stability and Capital Adequacy Board.

[31]See GAO-11-707.

the single pool of assets. The proposal also would give regulators a role in determining whether existing bankruptcy exclusions for insurance companies, broker-dealers, or commodity brokers should be maintained. The Hoover Institution resolution project group noted that these exclusions can complicate the resolution of a major financial institution, because the bankruptcy court can deal only with pieces of the firm.

Experts Noted Limited Effects on Regulator Roles from Most Proposals and Trade-offs Relating to Orderliness and Effectiveness

The experts at the first roundtable generally supported three of the four proposed changes to the role of regulators in bankruptcy proceedings, but noted that these proposals might have limited effects. None of the experts who responded to written questions indicated that requiring notice and consultation with regulators or granting regulators a right to be heard in bankruptcy court would greatly change the existing bankruptcy process. The experts noted that regulators already play these roles in financial company bankruptcies.

- In response to the proposal to require notice to regulators, the experts generally agreed that regulators and financial companies usually have a great deal of communication and involvement, particularly when an institution is experiencing financial difficulties. One expert worried that requiring notice to the regulator before filing for bankruptcy might allow regulators to prevent the debtor from filing and adversely affect recoveries for creditors.

- In relation to regulatory authority to compel involuntary filings, the experts who specifically addressed this proposal said that regulators already have ways of forcing a financial company to file for bankruptcy through their existing regulatory powers. A few experts said that regulators can use the threat of placing the firm into FDIC receivership under OLA if the firm does not file voluntarily for bankruptcy.[32] One expert expressed the view that once living wills are in place, regulators may compel a financial company to execute its resolution

---

[32]NAIC and state insurance officials noted that generally state insurance regulators place insurance companies into receivership. However, insurers can voluntarily request to be so placed. Under OLA, state insurance regulators retain this right. However, if an insurance company or subsidiary has been designated through OLA to go through the state's orderly resolution for insurance companies and the state insurance regulators have not taken action within 60 days of the designation, FDIC can stand in place of the insurance regulators to place the company into orderly liquidation under the state's laws.

plan by filing for voluntary bankruptcy.[33] Regulators also can take other actions. For example, under the statute, the Federal Reserve and FDIC may jointly take corrective action, including ultimately requiring the divestiture of certain assets, if they jointly determine that a firm has not been able to submit a plan that meets the statutory criteria.[34] Under SEC and CFTC rules, an undercapitalized securities broker-dealer or commodity broker cannot operate and must therefore be liquidated. One expert with whom we spoke said that even if regulators were given an explicit right to place a firm in involuntary bankruptcy, they would be unlikely to use that authority.

- In response to the proposal to give regulators an explicit right to be heard, experts who addressed the issue said regulators are routinely heard by the court in bankruptcy proceedings. And as noted previously, SEC and CFTC already have legal standing in some cases. Court officials said they were not aware of an instance in which a regulator was denied the right to be heard by the court. However, experts also said making this an express right might have benefits, which we discuss later in this report.

Although experts favored most of the regulatory proposals, they were opposed to having regulators decide whether a firm should be resolved on a consolidated basis and noted that these changes would undermine key legal and regulatory constructs. One expert noted that the idea undermined the concept of having corporate separateness for subsidiaries. Corporate separateness is generally the principle that a parent corporation is not liable for actions taken by its subsidiaries. Another expert noted that encouraging substantive consolidation as determined by the regulator could have a negative impact on the predictability and transparency of the bankruptcy process, detracting from

---

[33]Under the living wills provision of Title I of the Dodd-Frank Act and the implementing regulations, certain large complex financial companies must provide the Federal Reserve, FDIC, and FSOC with plans that detail how they could be resolved under the Code (or other applicable non-OLA regime) in a way that substantially mitigates the risk that the failure of the company would have serious adverse effects on financial stability in the United States. *See* Dodd-Frank Act § 165(d), 12 C.F.R. § 381.2(o).

[34]Dodd-Frank Act, Pub. L. No. 111-203, § 165(d)(5). If the Federal Reserve and FDIC determine that the plans are not credible or would not facilitate an orderly resolution under the Code, the agencies may impose more stringent capital, leverage or liquidity requirements or restrictions on the growth, activities, or operations of the company until an acceptable plan is submitted, or require divestiture of certain assets if no acceptable plan is submitted within 2 years.

the orderliness and effectiveness of that process. A third expert noted that treating the legal entities of a financial company in bankruptcy on a consolidated basis would conflict with the U.S. regulatory structure, which is designed around separate legal entities, such as depository institutions, broker-dealers, and insurance companies. However, companies continue to manage themselves along business lines that cut across legal entities. A regulatory expert said that removing the exemption for securities broker-dealers and commodity brokers from bankruptcy could undermine the purpose of the regulatory construct applied to those entities and the ability of regulators to protect customers' assets. An expert noted that overriding state insurance regulators could lead to intensive litigation. Additionally, NAIC and state insurance officials said that the priority structure for bankruptcy is inappropriate for insurers because the primary goal in the resolution of an insurance company is to protect the policyholders. Because of this, policyholders generally receive priority over creditors in an insurance receivership beyond any claims supported by collateral.

Experts at our roundtables also broadly discussed the proposals in relation to criteria for orderly and effective bankruptcies (including minimizing systemic risk and promoting due process). Most fundamentally, these experts had differing views on whether bankruptcy, as currently construed, was an appropriate vehicle for minimizing systemic risk. Some participants at the roundtable raised issues about whether the court could act quickly enough to stem systemic spillovers from the debtor company to other companies and markets. They noted other potential trade-offs. For example, to act quickly in cases involving large and complex financial companies, courts might need to shorten notice periods and limit parties' right to be heard, which could compromise due process and creditor rights. Similarly, one participant said that if the goal was to turn the Code into an effective resolution tool, the fundamental balance of power among debtor, creditor, and regulator might need to be altered. Another was concerned that if regulators become more involved in bankruptcy cases, courts might defer to them over other parties, undermining the ability of creditors to argue their cases. However, a legal expert at the roundtable doubted that the courts would be overly solicitous to regulators. Another legal expert noted that regulators could enhance due process by educating the court and providing a method for verifying information provided by the financial institution. One of these participants noted that standards for an involuntary bankruptcy initiated by the regulator might require a new definition for insolvency that would consider both regulatory and systemic interests.

Nevertheless, many of the experts indicated that regulatory involvement in bankruptcies was consistent with minimizing systemic risk. These experts said that regulators do and should have influence in times of crisis and that commencing a bankruptcy without regulatory involvement could be problematic. Additionally, some of the experts at the roundtable noted that regulators ought to have the power to compel a financial firm to file for bankruptcy because, as one regulatory expert said, allowing a financial firm to continue to do business when it is in vulnerable financial condition would likely add to concerns for systemic risk.

Experts Generally Agreed That Proposals Need Further Consideration

Although experts generally supported proposals to change the roles of regulators, they said implementing the proposals relating to notice and involuntary proceedings could be difficult. Experts at our roundtable said that determining the correct number of days for notification to the regulator would be difficult. For example, requiring a financial institution to provide notice to and consult with regulators 10 days in advance of filing for bankruptcy—the number of days specified in proposals introduced in the 111th Congress—might not work in practice. One expert said that 10 days can be a long time in a financial crisis. Another noted that the firm's need to file for bankruptcy might arise very quickly and that a firm might only be able to notify its regulator a day or two in advance of its filing. As an example, an expert noted the rapid collapse of the investment firm Bear Stearns and Co. In 2008, senior management of Bear Stearns gave the Federal Reserve Bank of New York a 1-day notification, saying that the company would file for bankruptcy protection the following day unless it received an emergency loan. In the failure of Lehman Brothers, the abruptness of the company's bankruptcy did not allow much time for attorneys to prepare for filing. Another expert said that a requirement to "notify and consult" with the regulator before entering bankruptcy should not interfere with the ability of a company to file for bankruptcy.

Determining which regulators to notify also may be difficult. Complex financial companies and their subsidiaries may have many regulators domestically and internationally. As a result, determining which regulator a bank holding company or nonbank financial company would notify if a domestic or foreign subsidiary were nearing insolvency is not clear. One expert noted that because large financial companies have many regulators, before a firm could file for bankruptcy it would be important to identify in advance which regulators to notify. Proposals introduced in the 111th Congress would have required that a nonbank financial company consult with its functional regulator, FSOC, and any agency charged with administering a nonbankruptcy insolvency regime for any component of the debtor firm, which could be a large number of regulators.[35] The proposals define functional regulator as the federal regulatory agency with the primary regulatory authority, such as an agency listed in section 509 of the Graham-Leach-Bliley Act. Some roundtable experts said that prebankruptcy consultation should be with the firm's primary regulator, although none of them defined this term.

FSOC—which under the Dodd-Frank Act is charged with identifying and responding to risks to U. S. financial stability—was included as a regulator in the notification and consultation proposal.[36] Treasury officials, including those who support FSOC, interpret the Dodd-Frank Act as having a preference for resolving financial companies through bankruptcy and said that FSOC has focused its activities on implementing its responsibilities under the act. Furthermore, in its annual reports FSOC has described the role that resolution plans are supposed to play in fostering orderly resolutions under the Code. Specifically, under the Dodd-Frank Act, bank holding companies with total consolidated assets of $50 billion or more and nonbank financial companies designated by FSOC for enhanced supervision by the Federal Reserve are required to submit resolution plans to the Federal Reserve, FDIC, and FSOC. FSOC's 2013 Annual Report included a recommendation that the Federal Reserve and FDIC implement their resolution plan authorities in a manner that better prepares firms and authorities for a rapid and orderly resolution under the Code.[37]

However, in our discussion with Treasury officials, including those who support FSOC, they noted that FSOC does not routinely evaluate

---

[35]*Bankruptcy Integrity and Accountability Act*, Senate Amendment 3832, 111th Cong., 2nd sess., Congressional Record (May 5, 2010): S3620-3624 and *Consumer Protection and Regulatory Enhancement Act*. HR 3310, 111th Cong., 1st sess., *Congressional Record* (July 24, 2009): E1964-E1967. Both proposals provided FSOC, or an entity with a similar conceptual function, the right to a prebankruptcy petition consultation. The House proposal referred to the similar agency with the conceptual function similar to FSOC as the Market Stability and Capital Adequacy Board.

[36]We have reported and testified before Congress on FSOC's management structure and mechanisms for meeting its mission. See GAO, *Financial Stability: New Counsel and Research Office Accountability and Transparency of Their Decisions* GAO-12-886 (Washington, D.C.: Sept. 11, 2012) and *Financial Stability: Continued Actions Needed to Strengthen New Counsel and Research Office* GAO-13-467T (Washington, D.C.: Mar. 14, 2013).

[37]See FSOC, *2012 Annual Report* (Washington, D.C.: July 2012).

GAO-13-622 Financial Company Bankruptcies

proposals that could alter the role of regulators in the bankruptcy process or other changes to the Code that might reduce systemic risk, such as narrowing the safe harbor treatment of QFCs. While current law does not specify a role for FSOC related to the potential filing of a bankruptcy by a systemically important financial company, when MF Global declared bankruptcy, FSOC met in emergency session to monitor the event and subsequently reported that the MF Global bankruptcy had not roiled markets.[38] Treasury officials and staff that support FSOC said that FSOC is focused on implementing provisions in the Dodd-Frank Act. Since helping to develop rules to implement OLA is explicit in the Dodd-Frank Act, FSOC has described activities related to these provisions and made recommendations—but has not considered the implications of changing the role of regulators under the Code. Although the Dodd-Frank Act does not amend the Code or explicitly call for FSOC to consider such changes, changing the role of regulators could potentially impact FSOC's ability to identify and respond to systemic risks in a timely fashion.

The roundtable experts noted that allowing financial regulators to initiate an involuntary bankruptcy for financial companies raised a number of implementation questions including appropriate time frames and standards. These experts generally agreed that lengthy time frames included in the rules for an involuntary bankruptcy filed by a creditor could reduce the value of a systemically important financial institution and endanger market stability.[39] However, one expert expressed concern over the possibility of regulators acting too quickly to place an institution in bankruptcy, especially during a financial crisis in which asset valuations might be in dispute. A legal expert noted that considering what the appropriate standard for placing a financial institution in bankruptcy would be was important. The expert noted the difficulty of distinguishing between an insolvent company and one experiencing temporary liquidity needs. Another expert proposed that a bankruptcy initiated by the regulator should require a standard similar to the standard in place for

---

[38]MF Global Holdings Ltd. and MF Global Finance USA Inc. filed on a consolidated basis for relief under Chapter 11 bankruptcy protection on October 31, 2011. The jointly registered broker-dealer and commodities broker subsidiaries of MF Global Holdings, operating as MF Global Inc., entered liquidation proceedings under SIPA.

[39]Debtors can defend against an involuntary proceeding including presenting objections within 21 days of being served the summons.

placing a firm in FDIC receivership under OLA.[40] The regulators at the roundtable thought that a regulatory framework that required firms to meet certain standards or be placed in bankruptcy—as currently exists for commodities brokers and securities broker-dealers—might alleviate some of the disadvantages posed by the creditor rules and would not necessarily require a change in the Code.

Experts Considered Funding Mechanisms Essential for Bankruptcies of Large Financial Companies

One criterion for an effective bankruptcy or resolution process is to limit taxpayer liability. Legislators have made proposals to limit the ability of the Treasury or the Federal Reserve to help finance bankruptcies of financial companies. For example, proposals introduced in the 111th Congress specifically would have forbidden the U.S. Treasury and Federal Reserve from participating in bankruptcy financing. However, some proposals recognize the difficulty of financing bankruptcies of large financial companies, especially during a crisis. The Chapter 14 proposal made by the Hoover Institution resolution project group would allow the government to provide subordinated DIP financing to companies with assets greater than $100 billion (subsidiaries included) with a hearing and the court's approval and oversight.[41] Experts at our roundtable discussed the appropriate role of the government in providing financing for firms in bankruptcy.

---

[40]The factors to be addressed are set forth in section 203(b) of the Dodd-Frank Act. Before the Secretary of the Treasury, in consultation with the President, makes a decision to seek the appointment of FDIC as receiver of a financial company, at least two-thirds of those serving on the Board of Governors of the Federal Reserve System and at least two-thirds of those serving on the Board of Directors of FDIC must vote to make a written recommendation to the Secretary of the Treasury to appoint FDIC as receiver. In the case of a broker-dealer, the recommendation must come from the Federal Reserve and SEC, in consultation with FDIC, and in the case of an insurance company from the Federal Reserve and the Director of the Federal Insurance Office, in consultation with FDIC.

[41]The DIP financer usually requires that its loan be secured with collateral and paid as an administrative expense of the estate, giving it priority over all prepetition creditors of the firm. Occasionally, such a loan is given priority over other administrative expenses. Such an arrangement is called a super priority. In contrast, a subordinated loan to a DIP would receive payment only after administrative expenses, other DIP lenders, and other creditors are paid.

Experts Considered Fully Secured Federal or Industry Funding Mechanisms Essential for Orderly and Efficient Bankruptcies

Experts at our roundtables emphasized that many of the proposals to make the bankruptcy process more orderly and effective depend on having an adequate funding mechanism. As a result, experts at the first roundtable generally agreed that changing the Code to prevent any federal funding of these bankruptcies would not be consistent with orderly and effective resolutions. In their written responses to a question asking what the most important changes would be to achieve most of the elements of an orderly and effective bankruptcy, experts most consistently responded that proposals to provide adequate funding, rather than to restrict it, were the most important changes that could be made. All but one of the eight experts responding put providing a funding source as the most important change to avoid fire sales. Experts said that support for federal funding rested on two propositions. First, voluntary private funding likely would be unavailable to finance the bankruptcy of a systemically important financial company. Second, the government should distinguish between funding for a bailout and funding that provided short-term liquidity.

Experts did not think that voluntary private funding would be available to finance a systemically important financial company because these companies are large and some of them grew substantially over the course of the financial crisis (see table 1). Solutions that were possible during the crisis, such as JPMorgan Chase providing funding for Bear Stearns, or Barclays' purchase of parts of Lehman, would be unlikely in the future because some firms have gotten much larger. Experts also noted that obtaining funding would be especially difficult during a period of general financial distress when firms large enough to provide funding might be experiencing difficulties themselves.

Table 1: Assets and Liabilities of Global Systemically Important Banking Institutions Headquartered in the United States, Fourth Quarter of 2007 and 2012

(U.S. dollars in millions)

Banking institutions	2007 Assets	2007 Liabilities	2012 Assets	2012 Liabilities
Bank of America Corp.	$1,720,688	$1,571,489	$2,212,004	$1,974,902
Bank of New York Mellon, Corp	197,839	168,269	359,301	321,858
Citigroup, Inc.	2,187,631	2,068,725	1,864,660	1,673,663
Goldman Sachs Group, Inc.	1,119,796	1,076,996	938,770	862,546
JPMorgan Chase & Co.	1,562,147	1,438,006	2,359,141	2,154,273
Morgan Stanley	1,045,409	1,014,140	780,960	711,223
State Street Corp.	142,937	131,628	222,229	201,358
Wells Fargo & Co.	575,442	527,528	1,422,968	1,264,057
Total	**$8,551,889**	**$7,996,781**	**$10,160,034**	**$9,163,880**

Source: GAO analysis of SEC and Federal Reserve data.

Note: These U.S. banking institutions were designated by the Financial Stability Board as of November 1, 2012. The board defines systemically important financial institutions as financial institutions whose distress or disorderly failure, because of their size, complexity and systemic interconnectedness, would cause significant disruption to the wider financial system and economic activity. Data are from December 2007 and December 2012 except for the 2007 assets and liabilities for Goldman Sachs Group, Inc. and Morgan Stanley. These data were reported in November 2007.

Several experts noted that any government funding would need to distinguish between bailing out an insolvent company, which they opposed, and providing short-term liquidity for a solvent company providing collateral, which they generally supported. One of the legal experts defined a bailout as the government putting in equity capital to support existing creditors. Legal and academic experts at our roundtables compared the provision of fully secured, liquidity funding with providing lender-of-last resort funding. They referred specifically to the Federal Reserve providing short-term liquidity through its discount window to solvent depository institutions with eligible collateral to secure the loan. The Federal Reserve accepts a very broad range of collateral to secure such loans.[42] Our roundtable experts generally agreed that funding for liquidity needs was essential and noted that in a period of financial distress the federal government might be the only entity with enough resources to provide such funding.

---

[42]See Federal Reserve, *Federal Reserve Collateral Guidelines*, www.frbdiscountwindow.org/FRcollguidelines.pdf, accessed on May 7, 2013.

GAO-13-622 Financial Company Bankruptcies

Although experts at the roundtables did not think voluntary private funding likely would be available for financing or other liquidity support during the bankruptcy of a large financial company, they did consider whether the industry as a whole might provide such support. They noted several options for such funding.

- The industry could create a fund or mechanism for providing liquidity to firms that needed it.

- The government could assess companies prior to a bankruptcy as it does for the deposit insurance fund.

- The government could raise funds through postbankruptcy assessments, while meeting immediate needs through temporary federal funding as with the Orderly Liquidation Fund under Title II of the Dodd-Frank Act. Under OLA, the Treasury may make funds available through an Orderly Liquidation Fund to FDIC as the receiver of a covered financial company.[43]

A few of the experts noted that some government guarantees might facilitate private-sector financing.

As with many of the proposals, our roundtable experts noted that implementing a proposal to allow fully secured federal funding for liquidity needs raised some difficulties. First, they noted the difficulty of distinguishing between an insolvent company and one experiencing temporary liquidity needs. This distinction is particularly difficult in a period of financial stress when valuation of assets may be difficult. For example, the value of some of Lehman Brothers Holding, Inc.'s (LBHI) real estate assets has increased since the time of its bankruptcy in 2008.

Second, experts at the first roundtable noted that the Dodd-Frank Act amendments to section 13(3) of the Federal Reserve Act might apply to some Federal Reserve funding related to a bankruptcy.[44] This provision

---

[43]If income from the liquidated assets of the financial company is insufficient to repay the borrowings, the FDIC may, if necessary, impose assessments on certain financial companies.

[44]Section 1101 of the Dodd-Frank Act provides that these emergency lending programs under section 13(3) of the Federal Reserve Act are not available to borrowers that are insolvent, which is defined to include entities that are in bankruptcy. See 12 U.S.C. § 343(B)(ii).

restricts the Federal Reserve from providing funding to a single distressed company but would allow it to provide funding to the financial system. Similar funding provided under the Primary Dealer Credit Facility in September 2008 (prior to the Dodd-Frank Act amendments), allowed Lehman Brothers, Inc. (LBI)—the broker-dealer and commodity broker subsidiary of LBHI—to remain a going concern after LBHI declared bankruptcy, thus facilitating the transfer of some assets to Barclays later that week. The remaining parts of LBI were liquidated in a SIPA proceeding. Under the terms of the loans provided through the Primary Dealer Credit Facility, the Federal Reserve Bank of New York became a secured creditor of the firm, giving it higher priority in the event of a bankruptcy. We found in 2011 that LBI and Barclays had repaid their overnight loans with interest, according to Federal Reserve officials. One legal and financial expert suggested that the Federal Reserve would be in compliance with the amendments to section 13(3) if it set up a fund for firms being resolved under the Code for large financial companies.

Third, experts noted that determining what types of assets firms could use to collateralize government or industry funding might be difficult. Although the Federal Reserve had accepted assets with significant tail risk (the probability of a rare event occurring that would result in great losses) as collateral during the crisis, experts noted that such risky assets might not be acceptable in the future.

Roundtable Experts Were Concerned about Using Federal Funding for Preferences to Some Creditors

We asked the experts at our first roundtable to discuss the advantages and disadvantages of the proposal made by the Hoover Institution resolution project group that calls for using subordinated government debt to provide payments to certain short-term creditors early in a bankruptcy proceeding. Such subordinated loans would be repaid with a lower priority than that of other creditors. The proposal further proposes a "claw-back" procedure if the preferred creditors have received more than they were entitled to when the reorganization or liquidation is finalized. The proposal was made to stem systemic concerns—the failure at one financial company spreading to others because short-term creditors would not have access to funds. Reliance on short-term funding exacerbated the financial crisis of 2007-2009.[45] And as has been noted by some Federal Reserve officials, regulatory reform has not yet addressed the risks to financial stability posed by short-term wholesale funding.[46]

Legal experts at the roundtable agreed that such payments could be made by treating certain short-term creditors as critical vendors during first-day motions. However, experts who discussed this issue at the first roundtable said that making decisions about providing funding to certain short-term creditors during a bankruptcy was not the best way to address systemic concerns associated with short-term liquidity. They noted that such a proposal would increase uncertainty for creditors during a bankruptcy proceeding. Two experts noted that they would not want to use subordinated federal funding. Another explained that the point of subordinating the funding is to help ensure that the government uses such funding to address concerns about liquidity rather than to defray certain creditors' losses. However, such funding would expose taxpayers to potential liability.

Instead, those experts who discussed this proposal at the first roundtable said that changing the Code to give an explicit priority to short- over long-term creditors would be preferable. They noted that an explicit priority would be a better option in that it would help to address systemic risk and lead to a more predictable bankruptcy process. In addition, such a priority might provide an incentive for firms to continue to provide short-term funding when a financial company experiences distress. One legal expert noted that the special bankruptcy laws for railroads had a provision that any creditor providing funding in the 6 months leading up to a bankruptcy

---

[45]For example, in GAO-11-707, we found that Lehman faced a liquidity crisis just prior to declaring bankruptcy when banks refused to lend money for its brokerage and other services. As a result, Lehman had difficulty rolling over borrowings of about $100 billion dollars every day to pay off maturing commercial paper and other commitments. More generally, when questions about the quality of subprime mortgages arose, investors became unwilling to make loans secured by a wide range of assets. When they could not borrow to meet their obligations, financial institutions were forced to sell assets, putting additional downward pressure on asset prices. As a result, some financial institutions had to put up more collateral and further mark down asset values leading to further intertwined downward spirals in asset and funding markets.

[46]Daniel K. Tarullo, "Evaluating Progress in Regulatory Reforms to Promote Financial Stability, (speech at the Peterson Institute for International Economics, Washington, D.C., May 3, 2013) and William C. Dudley, "Fixing Wholesale Funding to Build a More Stable Financial System," (speech at the New York Bankers Association's 2013 Annual Meeting and Economic Forum, New York, N.Y., Feb. 1, 2013).

had priority over other creditors in that bankruptcy proceeding. This type of provision might have created an incentive to provide funding to a railroad experiencing short-term financing issues and thus, might have prevented a bankruptcy. However, a legal expert at our second roundtable said that this would create unfair treatment for creditors providing long-term financing, because long- and short-term creditors were members of the same creditor class.

While a priority for short- over long-term creditors might reduce the incentive to withdraw funding leading up to a bankruptcy and reduce the likelihood of systemic issues associated with liquidity shortages during a bankruptcy, it could have additional consequences. For example, such a priority would provide more of an incentive for creditors to provide short- rather than long-term funding. If there were less likelihood that these short-term creditors would lose their funds in the case of a default because they had priority over other creditors, they might be less likely to monitor the credit-worthiness of borrowers. As a result, the market might be less likely to discipline companies that take on excessive risk. Although promoting market discipline is not among the criteria we identified for orderly and effective bankruptcies, it is a goal of the Dodd-Frank Act.

Experts Had Varying Views on Advantages and Disadvantages of QFC Proposals

Experts at our roundtables evaluated proposals to change the treatment of certain QFCs relative to criteria for orderly and effective financial company bankruptcies. Specifically, they discussed the effects of proposals for removing all safe harbors for QFCs; partially rolling back safe harbors on specific contracts; implementing a temporary stay for all or certain contracts; and allowing trustees to "avoid" contracts entered into within specified periods prior to the bankruptcy filing if they are determined to be preferential or fraudulent.[47] The experts generally agreed that limiting safe-harbor treatment would affect derivative and repurchase agreement markets and could limit short-term funding options for financial companies especially in periods of distress. However, the experts had differing views on the advantages and disadvantages of the

---

[47]Trustees can avoid contracts entered into in the 90 days prior to a bankruptcy if they are determined to be preferential; up to two years prior to a bankruptcy if they are determined to be fraudulent. We provided the experts with another proposal—keeping contracts open after bankruptcy with revaluations determined by the courts—but experts did not address it, so it is not included in this discussion.

proposals, and those views are still evolving as lessons learned from the treatment of these contracts during the Lehman Brothers bankruptcy remain unclear.

Experts Generally Agreed That Limiting Safe-Harbor Treatment of QFCs Would Affect Markets and Funding Availability

The roundtable experts generally agreed that limiting the safe-harbor treatment—removing it all together or providing it to a more limited set of contracts—would reduce the use of derivatives and repurchase agreements. Some experts have noted that these markets grew substantially after additional types of contracts were granted safe-harbor treatment in 2005 (see fig. 2). However, one expert we spoke with noted that in his opinion the industry has tended to overstate the impact that limiting the safe harbors would have on the size of the markets, which the expert thought would likely be minimal.

Figure 2: Primary Dealer Repurchase Agreements and Global Over-the-Counter Derivatives Markets, 2000 to 2012

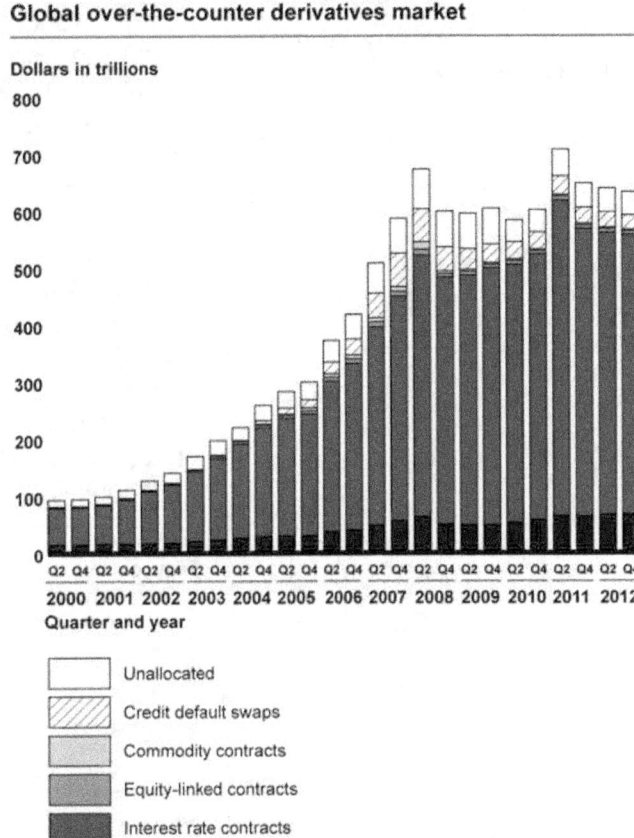

Source: FSOC 2013 Annual Report, Bank for International Settlements (right chart).

Several of the roundtable experts thought that if downsizing these markets was a goal, it should be done directly through regulations rather than through changes in the Code. For example, the experts noted that derivatives markets have been undergoing vast change as a result of requirements in the Dodd-Frank Act (such as requiring certain contracts to be tracked more effectively and traded on exchanges). However, another expert noted that it would be good if the Code were consistent with regulatory goals. Limiting the safe harbors would reduce the availability of short-term funding for financial companies. Short-term funding for financial companies creates flexibility, but, at the same time, it sets the stage for potential runs on firms.

Experts Held Varying Views on Proposal Impacts Relative to Orderliness and Effectiveness

As figure 3 shows, there was little consensus in written responses provided by our roundtable experts on how, if at all, changes in QFC treatment under the Code would affect the orderliness and effectiveness of financial company bankruptcies (see app. II for more detailed information on the proposals).[48] However, most of our roundtable experts responded that removing all of the safe harbors would detract from orderliness and effectiveness and none of them responded that this would greatly enhance orderliness and effectiveness. For the other proposals, the experts were split fairly evenly in their written responses between those who thought the proposal would enhance the orderliness and effectiveness and those who thought it would detract from orderliness and effectiveness. Many of the experts who thought allowing trustees to "avoid" contracts would detract from orderly and effective bankruptcies chose "greatly detract." Generally, those experts representing industry interests noted that the proposals would detract from orderliness and effectiveness, and those in favor of adopting certain proposals thought that industry opposition would be difficult to overcome.

Figure 3: Expert's Evaluation of How QFC Proposals Would Affect Orderliness and Effectiveness of Financial Company Bankruptcies, 2013

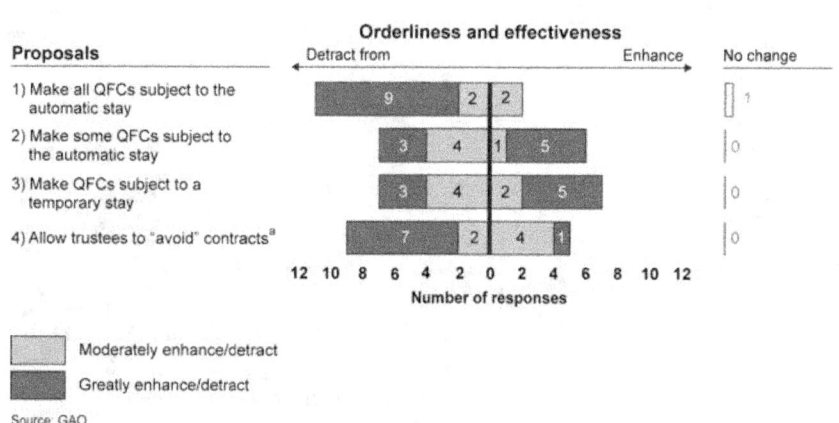

Source: GAO.

[a]Trustees' generally can "avoid" contracts entered into in the 90 days prior to a bankruptcy if they are determined to be preferential; up to 2 years prior to a bankruptcy if they are determined to be fraudulent.

---

[48]We provided the experts with another proposal on keeping contracts open after bankruptcy with revaluations determined by the courts but experts spent almost no time addressing it so it is not included in this discussion.

Experts at the roundtable noted that even if there was high-level agreement on what changes to the Code were needed, legal experts might disagree on the precise details. For example, with regard to the safe-harbor exemptions from avoidance actions—trustees' ability to "avoid" transfers entered into in the 90 days prior to a bankruptcy if they are determined to be preferential or up to 2 years prior to a bankruptcy if they are determined to be fraudulent—some legal experts at the second roundtable said that the courts were giving preferential treatment to contracts that in principle should not be receiving it. Specifically, they said that the courts were interpreting section 546(e) of the Code in a way that allows contracts that otherwise might be considered preferential or fraudulent to remain in force.[49] As a result, they noted that changes to the Code might be made to tighten that section. For example, a roundtable expert said that section 546(e) of the Code should be changed so that fictional transactions, such as Ponzi scheme payments, would not receive such treatment.[50] Another legal expert cited a number of cases in which contracts entered into within 90 days prior to the bankruptcy filing, which would be considered preferential without the safe-harbor exemption, were being given safe-harbor treatment. For example, in the bankruptcy case of communications company Quebecor, insurance companies that held private placement notes that qualified for safe-harbor treatment had received 105 cents on the dollar while other unsecured creditors received

---

[49]Section 546(e) states, with certain exceptions, the trustee may not avoid a transfer that is a margin payment or settlement payment made by or to a commodity broker, forward contract merchant, stockbroker, financial institution, financial participant, or securities clearing agency, or that is a transfer made by or to one of the entities listed above in connection with a securities contract, commodity contract, or forward contract made before the bankruptcy.

[50]See for example, *Picard v. Katz*, 462 B.R. 447, 451-52 (S.D.N.Y. 2011).

a fraction of a dollar.[51] The expert and others said that it might be useful to allow a judge to make decisions relative to some contracts. However, one expert at the roundtable noted that this could be a very long, complex process. In addition, allowing the judge to decide which contracts would get safe-harbor treatment when counterparties defaulted would increase the uncertainty attached to those contracts.

Our roundtable experts also varied in their evaluations of the proposals relative to some of the specific criteria we had identified for orderliness and effectiveness such as limiting systemic risk, avoiding fire sales, maximizing value, and preserving due process.

Limiting Systemic Risk and Avoiding Fire Sales

When explicitly asked, some experts responded that limiting the safe harbors would increase systemic risk, while others responded that limiting them would reduce it. Such a dichotomy could result from differences in the way the experts viewed markets.[52] Having the safe harbors likely increases dependence on short-term funding and thus increases the chance for a run if questions arise about a company's financial soundness. In addition, needing to sell off assets because of a lack of funding could lead to a spiral of falling asset prices. However, safe harbors are also thought to limit systemic effects before and during a bankruptcy. According to an expert at the second roundtable, if counterparties are certain about the safe-harbor treatment of their contracts, such treatment may limit runs prior to bankruptcy because counterparties know they will be able to terminate or liquidate their

---

[51]In September 2012, the District Court upheld a Bankruptcy Court ruling that Quebecor's payment of more than $376 million to purchase and redeem a series of private placement notes that an affiliated company had issued years earlier were settlement payments. *In re: Quebecor World (USA) Inc.*, 480 B.R. 468 (S.D.N.Y. 2012). By being deemed settlement payments, the money was protected by the § 546(e) safe harbor which prevented the bankruptcy estate from pulling the money back into the estate and permitted the note holders to retain the money they had been paid. This decision was based on an earlier decision in the Enron case. In the June 2011 Enron decision, the Appeals Court determined that Enron's payments to certain companies to retire specific commercial paper prior to its maturity was within the § 546(e) safe harbor because they were settlement payments. Thus, Enron's trustees could not have the commercial paper holders return that money to the Enron estate. *In re: Enron Creditors Recovery Corp.*, 651 F.3d 329 (2011). The Quebecor District Court decision was upheld by the Appeals Court in June 2013. *In re: Quebecor World (USA) Inc.*, 2013 U.S. App. LEXIS 11615 (2d App., June 10, 2013).

[52]Mark J. Roe, "The Derivatives Market's Payment Priorities as Financial Crisis Accelerator," *Stanford Law Review*, Vol. 63, no. 3 (March 2011).

positions in case of default. In addition, the safe harbors primarily exist to limit market turmoil during a bankruptcy—that is, they are to prevent the insolvency of one firm from spreading to other firms and possibly threatening the collapse of an affected market. Although FSOC has reported on threats to financial stability from derivative and repurchase agreement markets, as with proposals to change regulators' roles under the Code, they have not considered the implications of potential changes to the safe-harbor treatment of these contracts during bankruptcy.

The roundtable experts made a number of specific points relative to the impact of QFC treatment on systemic risk and fire sales of assets. One expert at the second roundtable noted that during the early days of the Lehman Bankruptcy, he thought that the QFC terminations would lead to a systemic event in derivatives markets, but that did not happen. The expert questioned whether the lack of a systemic event reflected Lehman's small share of the market—5 percent—or the safe-harbor protection. In contrast, the commercial paper market did experience a systemic event—becoming illiquid after the Lehman bankruptcy. However, another participant noted that it was not the claims process in a bankruptcy that caused systemic risk; it was the uncertainty, the effect on counterparties, and market reactions. Roundtable participants also discussed the likelihood that safe-harbor treatment or bankruptcy in general could create asset fire sales. One expert noted that fire sales were more likely to occur in the period leading up to bankruptcy rather than after the bankruptcy was filed. Another industry expert noted that some unpublished research suggests that fire sales of Lehman's assets that might have resulted from the treatment of QFCs did not take place following the bankruptcy filing. Instead, counterparties terminated only those contracts that had maintained their value.

Maximizing Value

Roundtable experts noted that conflicts might arise depending on whether the goal of a bankruptcy proceeding was to maximize value for the economy, for the debtors, or for the creditors. One legal expert noted that in a time of financial crisis, balancing market expectations and needs against the needs of an individual company was difficult. Debtors usually are expected to fare best when companies can be reorganized under Chapter 11. Under Chapter 11, the purpose of the automatic stay is to preserve the value of companies while debtors consider their options. However, one roundtable expert noted that with the rapid dissolution of value for a financial company as a result of the safe harbors, liquidation is a more likely outcome than reorganization. Another expert noted that even if QFCs were stayed, value could dissipate quickly in financial company bankruptcies because that value rests on the confidence of the debtors' counterparties. In addition, one expert raised concern about the impact of the safe harbors on the remaining value for creditors after QFC positions were terminated. In a bankruptcy, creditors compete with counterparties to derivative contracts and repurchase agreements for a firm's assets. Allowing the QFCs to be terminated while other debts are stayed means there are fewer assets available for those creditors. However, since creditors know that they are less well protected in bankruptcy, they should command a higher price for the risk they are taking when they provide credit. So, determining whether creditors are being disadvantaged overall is difficult.

Roundtable participants also discussed whether a temporary stay for QFCs would enhance the value of a financial company; however, as noted earlier, they were split on whether this would contribute or detract from the overall orderliness and effectiveness of financial company bankruptcies. For example, while several experts said that a temporary stay might facilitate a sale of a company's derivatives to a third party, the sale would increase concentration in the market and ultimately contribute to greater overall systemic risk. Other experts agreed that a temporary stay would be useful only to the extent that an exit strategy, such as selling to a third-party buyer, was available or a bridge company—which is a temporary company used to maintain the failed company's operations—could be constructed. These experts cited the case of General Motors as an example of what they were suggesting. However, the newly formed company in the case of General Motors was not temporary. In contrast, one expert presented a hypothetical example that did not involve a sale of the whole entity to a third party or the construction of a bridge company. In this example the judge would have from a 10 to 12 day stay, which might allow the judge to dispose of pieces of the company, leaving a small enough entity that its assets could be liquidated through normal bankruptcy proceedings. However, other experts noted that it might be difficult to determine what the appropriate number of days for a temporary stay might be.

Maintaining Due Process and Providing Certainty

Several of the experts at our roundtables questioned whether bankruptcy reforms designed to deal with systemically important financial companies would adequately protect due process given the need to move quickly in such a bankruptcy. They suggested that due process might be compromised or would depend on the ability of counterparties and creditors to take action after regulators or courts make decisions (as is the case with OLA). For example, if preferences were given to some counterparties or creditors during a temporary stay, other counterparties or creditors would have the right to take action to recover value or "claw back" value later in the process, as opposed to having a judge consider the views of all of the parties prior to making any decisions.

Roundtable experts noted that some changes to the Code relative to the treatment of QFCs could create uncertainty in the process. Specifically, counterparties need certainty about bankruptcy treatment when they enter a contract. To provide that certainty, several experts agreed that changes should be detailed in the terms of the contract rather than determined at the time of the bankruptcy. However, one of the experts noted that even with provisions specified in the Code, counterparties might still be uncertain for some time about how certain contracts would be treated. Although the Code had been amended in 2005 to extend safe-harbor treatments to more types of repurchase agreements, that expert said that uncertainty as to how the courts would treat repurchase agreements contributed to the Lehman Brothers bankruptcy. Leading up to the bankruptcy, counterparties were unwilling to extend new short-term funding because of the uncertainty—essentially precipitating a run on the firm.

Our roundtable experts noted other issues that would arise relative to making any changes in the Code, such as whether contracts that already existed would be processed under the Code at that time or under the new Code. One expert said that contracts should be grandfathered, while another pointed out that the grandfathered contracts might be around for another 30 years, creating other difficulties. While it is difficult to assess how many contracts would be long term, key contracts are thought to be used for overnight funding. When the 2005 changes were made to expand the contracts receiving safe-harbor treatment, the new treatment applied to all contracts, including those that had been entered into prior to that time. Some roundtable experts further suggested that not knowing which judge will have a case and how that judge will make decisions can introduce additional uncertainty into the treatment of certain contracts.

Not knowing whether a qualified financial contract would be subject to the Code or OLA creates further uncertainty about how a contract will be treated. Under the latter, FDIC becomes the receiver of the company and QFCs are stayed for 1 business day. During that day, FDIC has an opportunity to transfer a company's derivatives to a third-party or bridge company. Under OLA, FDIC can choose to transfer contracts with one company to the bridge company while choosing not to transfer those with another company. However, if FDIC chooses to transfer a contract with a specific company, it would have to transfer all of the contracts with that company.[53] There was some presumption among roundtable participants that very large systemically important institutions would be resolved under OLA rather than through bankruptcy. However, FDIC officials testified before the Subcommittee on Oversight and Investigations of the House Committee on Financial Services in April 2013 that under the Dodd-Frank Act, bankruptcy is the preferred resolution framework in the event of a failure of a systemically important financial company.[54]

Experts Noted That Lessons Learned from Lehman Bankruptcy Are Still Unclear

Experts at our roundtable said that the lessons learned from the Lehman bankruptcy that might be applied in considering changes to the safe harbors are still unclear. Early reports and statements about the LBHI bankruptcy said that in the first 5 weeks after LBHI filed for bankruptcy, approximately 80 percent of its derivatives counterparties terminated contracts that were not subject to the automatic stay.[55] However, some of the initial counterparty claims have been found to have been overstated. Two experts at our second roundtable specifically noted that the large initial loss in value was, in part, the result of LBHI counterparties' initially overstating their claims against LBHI, and subsequently some of these claims have been overturned in adversary proceedings. For example, Swedbank AB, a Swedish bank, that was a creditor of LBHI, sought to offset Lehman's payment obligations under prepetition swaps with deposits Lehman had made at Swedbank after filing for bankruptcy. The Bankruptcy Court of the Southern District of New York ruled against Swedbank, holding that the post petition deposits could not be used to offset prepetition swaps.[56] In another proceeding involving the Lehman

---

[53]If FDIC chooses not to transfer a contract with a specific company, none of the contracts with that company may be transferred.

[54]FDIC, *Statement of Federal Deposit Insurance Corporation on Who Is Too Big To Fail? Examining the Application of Title I of the Dodd-Frank Act* (Washington D.C.: Apr. 16, 2013).

[55]See appendix III for information on how qualified contracts may be liquidated, terminated, or accelerated under the Code.

[56]In re Lehman Bros. Holdings, Inc., 433 B.R. 101(Bankr. S.D. N.Y. 2010) ("Memorandum Decision Granting Debtors' Motion Pursuant to Sections 105(a) and 362 of the Bankruptcy Code for an Order Enforcing the Automatic Stay Against and Compelling Payment of Post-Petition Funds by Swedbank AB"). The decision said that the payments lacked mutuality.

bankruptcy, a lender, Bank of America, seized the debtor's account funds, which were unrelated to any safe-harbor transaction, to set off certain contracts that could receive safe-harbor treatment. The court ruled that the bank's use of the funds to set off the transactions violated the automatic stay.[57] Further, some experts no longer supported proposals they had originally made in response to Lehman's early perceived losses.

As a result, experts continue to weigh whether changes to the treatment of derivatives and repurchase agreements under the Code are needed. The Hoover Institution resolution project group continues to discuss their proposals and plans to issue additional publications on their Chapter 14 proposals. The American Bankruptcy Institute has a Commission to Study the Reform of Chapter 11 and has appointed advisory committees to consider various aspects, including the treatment of QFCs. Its work is expected to continue for some time. Throughout the roundtable discussion, the participants noted that changes to the Code should not be made without considering ongoing changes in the broader legal and regulatory environment for derivatives. Specifically, they noted that the Dodd-Frank Act calls for a number of significant changes in the regulation of derivatives that are still being implemented, and the industry is looking at potential changes to derivatives contracts. Finally, experts noted the need to make changes consistently across international borders, especially in the United States and United Kingdom. During the Lehman Brothers bankruptcy, differences in the treatment of various contracts caused courts in the United States and United Kingdom to rule in opposing ways on the same contracts.

Conclusions

The financial crisis and the failures of some large financial companies raised questions about the adequacy of the Code for effectively reorganizing or liquidating these companies without causing further harm to the financial system. Although the Dodd-Frank Act created OLA, an alternative resolution process, filing for bankruptcy under the Code remains the preferred resolution mechanism even for systemically important financial companies. Some proposals to modify the Code recognize that currently the Code may not adequately address threats to financial stability. Some proposals—changing the role of regulators in the

---

[57]Bank of America, N.A. v. Lehman Brothers Holdings, Inc., 439 B.R. 811 (Bankr. S.D. N.Y. 2010).

bankruptcy process, creating funding mechanisms, and limiting the safe-harbor treatment of qualified financial contracts—may address this potential shortcoming. However, experts are not ready to recommend specific changes to the Code and the proposals require further consideration. FSOC—which was established under the Dodd-Frank Act to identify and respond to threats to financial stability—has not specifically considered changes to the role of regulators in bankruptcy or the treatment of QFCs. Although the Dodd-Frank Act does not explicitly require FSOC to assess changes to the Code, it is well positioned to take a broad view of potential changes within the context of other regulatory and market changes prescribed by the act. It is also well positioned to decide the appropriate level of attention such changes merit. Such attention to the systemic implications of financial company bankruptcies could improve FSOC's ability to take timely and effective action to identify and respond to threats to U.S. financial stability.

Recommendations for Executive Action

To fulfill FSOC's role under the Dodd-Frank Act to identify and respond to threats to financial stability, we recommend that the Secretary of the Treasury, as Chairperson of FSOC, in consultation with other FSOC members, consider the implications for U.S. financial stability of changing the role of regulators and narrowing the safe harbor treatment of qualified financial contracts in financial company bankruptcies.

Agency Comments

We provided a draft of this report to AOUSC, CFTC, FDIC, the Federal Reserve, NAIC, the Departments of the Treasury and Justice, and SEC, for review and comment. CFTC, FDIC, NAIC, and SEC provided technical comments, which we have incorporated as appropriate. AOUSC, the Federal Reserve, and Department of Justice did not provide comments. Treasury's Under Secretary for Domestic Finance, on behalf of the Chairperson of FSOC, provided written comments, which are reprinted in appendix IV.

In commenting on our draft report, FSOC said that it shares our concern that a disorderly financial company bankruptcy could pose risks to financial stability. However, FSOC stated that it would be premature for FSOC to prioritize the consideration of proposals to amend the Code until the Dodd-Frank Act is fully implemented or there is evidence of risks that cannot be adequately addressed within existing law. FSOC added that the Federal Reserve Board and FDIC are currently implementing provisions of the Dodd-Frank Act requiring designated financial companies to submit resolution plans ("living wills") to facilitate their orderly resolution under the Code. FSOC also noted that it is facilitating communication and coordination on the implementation of OLA and living will requirements. FSOC noted further that the council is engaged in a variety of other actions to address risks to financial stability posed by the failure of one or more financial companies such as the designation of nonbank financial companies.

We acknowledge FSOC's efforts to implement the Dodd-Frank Act and the actions they have taken to address risks to financial stability, including some actions related to implementing OLA. However, rather than considering changes to the Code after the Dodd-Frank Act is fully implemented, our recommendation is intended to encourage FSOC to actively address such changes in conjunction with these efforts—particularly as some suggested changes would affect regulators' and ultimately FSOC's ability to respond to the failure of a large complex institution. First, changing the role of regulators in a financial company bankruptcy could be critical for effective resolution. For example, the point at which regulators become aware of an impending or actual financial company bankruptcy could be critical to determining whether its living will could be used to improve the orderliness and effectiveness of the bankruptcy. Similarly, timing could be critical in determining whether to use OLA, which is to be used if a bankruptcy under the Code were determined to have serious adverse effects on U.S. financial stability. Second, narrowing the treatment of QFCs could also have implications for limiting systemic risk. As some members of the council have stated publicly, bankruptcy remains the preferred method for resolving failing financial companies. Given that preference and FSOC's charge to identify and respond to risks to U.S. financial stability, our recommendation—that FSOC consider the implications for U.S. financial stability of changing the role of regulators and narrowing safe harbor treatment of QFCs in financial company bankruptcies—is consistent with its statutory role and responsibilities.

We are sending copies of this report to the appropriate congressional committees, the Director of the Administrative Office of the U.S. Courts, Chairman of the Commodity Futures Trading Commission, Attorney General, Secretary of the Treasury, Chairman of the Federal Deposit Insurance Corporation, Director of the Federal Judicial Center, Chairman of the Board of Governors of the Federal Reserve System, Chief Executive Officer of the National Association of Insurance Commissioners, Chairman of the Securities and Exchange Commission, and other interested parties. The report also is available at no charge on the GAO website at http://www.gao.gov.

If you or your staff members have any questions about this report, please contact Alicia Puente Cackley at (202) 512-8678 or cackleya@gao.gov. Contact points for our Offices of Congressional Relations and Public Affairs may be found on the last page of this report. Major contributors to this report are listed in appendix V.

Alicia Puente Cackley
Director
Financial Markets and Community Investment

List of Committees

The Honorable Tim Johnson
Chairman
The Honorable Mike Crapo
Ranking Member
Committee on Banking, Housing, and Urban Affairs
United States Senate

The Honorable Patrick J. Leahy
Chairman
The Honorable Charles E. Grassley
Ranking Member
Committee on the Judiciary
United States Senate

The Honorable Jeb Hensarling
Chairman
The Honorable Maxine Waters
Ranking Member
Committee on Financial Services
House of Representatives

The Honorable Robert W. Goodlatte
Chairman
The Honorable John Conyers, Jr.
Ranking Member
Committee on the Judiciary
House of Representatives

Appendix I: Objectives, Scope, and Methodology

Section 202(e) of the Dodd-Frank Wall Street Reform and Consumer Protection Act (Dodd-Frank Act) mandated that we report on the orderliness and efficiency of financial company bankruptcies every year for 3 years after passage of the act, in the fifth year, and every 5 years thereafter.[1] This report, the third in the series, examines the advantages and disadvantages of certain proposals to modify the Bankruptcy Code (Code) for financial company bankruptcies. Specifically this report examines the advantages and disadvantages of proposals (1) to change the role of financial regulators in the bankruptcy process; (2) affecting the funding of financial company bankruptcies; and (3) to change the safe-harbor treatment of qualified financial contracts (QFC), including derivatives and repurchase agreements.

To address all of our objectives, we reviewed relevant laws, including the Code and the Dodd-Frank Act as well as GAO reports that addressed bankruptcy issues and financial institution failures. We specifically reviewed the reports we issued during the first 2 years of the mandate as well as reports written under the same or similar mandates by the Administrative Office of the United States Courts (AOUSC) and the Board of Governors of the Federal Reserve System (Federal Reserve).[2] We also updated our review of published economic and legal research on the effectiveness of bankruptcies that we had originally completed during the first year of the mandate. For the original search we relied on Internet search databases (including EconLit and Proquest) to identify studies published or issued after 2000 up through 2010. We reviewed these articles to further determine the extent to which they were relevant to our engagement, that is, whether they discussed criteria for effectiveness of the bankruptcy process, key features of the bankruptcy process, or

---

[1]Pub. L. No. 111-203, § 202(e). The Administrative Office of the U.S. Courts (AOUSC) is also required to address Pub. L. No. 111-203, § 202(e) on the same time frame. The Board of Governors of the Federal Reserve System (Federal Reserve) was required to address a similar mandate—Pub. L. No. 111-203, § 216—in July 2011.

[2]GAO, *Bankruptcy: Complex Financial Institutions and International Coordination Pose Challenges*, GAO-11-707 (Washington, D.C.: July 19, 2011) and *Bankruptcy: Agencies Continue Rulemakings for Clarifying Specific Provisions of Orderly Liquidation Authority*, GAO-12-735 ((Washington, D.C.: July 12, 2012); AOUSC, *Report Pursuant to Section 202(e) of the Dodd-Frank Wall Street Reform and Consumer Protection Act of 2010*, (Washington, D.C.: July 2011) and *Second Report Pursuant to Section 202(e) of the Dodd-Frank Wall Street Reform and Consumer Protection Act of 2010, Pub. L. No. 111-203 (2010)*, (Washington, D.C.: July 2012); and Federal Reserve, *Study on the Resolution of Financial Companies under the Bankruptcy Code* (Washington, D.C.: July 2011).

proposals for improving the bankruptcy process. We augmented this
Internet search with articles provided by those we interviewed or obtained
from conferences. In addition, we reviewed a number of prior GAO
reports on financial institutions and the financial crisis. For this report, we
replicated the literature search for 2011 and 2012. Further we met with
officials at the following federal government agencies: AOUSC; the
Commodity Futures Trading Commission; Federal Deposit Insurance
Corporation; Department of Justice; Department of the Treasury,
including officials who support the Financial Stability Oversight Council
(FSOC); Federal Reserve; and Securities and Exchange Commission. In
addition we met with officials of the National Association of Insurance
Commissioners and members of insurance departments in Illinois, Iowa,
and Texas.

We relied on our earlier work and the updated literature review to
establish criteria for orderliness and effectiveness and to develop a list of
proposals related to the role of regulators in the bankruptcy process or
the role of government in financing bankruptcies, as well as proposals to
change the safe-harbor treatment of certain financial contracts. In our
earlier work, we analyzed the results of the literature review and expert
interviews to determine criteria for orderliness and effectiveness of
financial company bankruptcies. These criteria are minimizing systemic
risk, avoiding fire sales, maximizing value; preserving due process, and
minimizing taxpayer liability. In that work, we also used the literature
review to determine the range of proposals that had been made to reform
the bankruptcy process for financial institutions. We categorized some of
the proposals into groups, such as those that included a role for the
regulators or modified the treatment of qualified financial contracts, and
then asked the experts looking at these categories and specific proposals
to tell us which they considered had merit and should be included for
further consideration and why. We also updated the literature review to
determine whether earlier proposals had evolved, proposals had been
subject to critical review, or additional proposals had been made. As we
had for our earlier work, we surveyed relevant government agencies for
information on newer studies they had or were conducting or were aware
of related to our objectives.

To obtain expert views on existing proposals and how these proposals
might be improved, we convened two roundtables to discuss the
advantages and disadvantages of specific proposals. The roundtables
were held at the National Academy of Sciences (NAS) and staff at NAS
assisted with determining who would sit on the roundtables. Generally,
roundtable members were chosen for their expertise on bankruptcy and

financial institutions and markets. We also discussed potential experts for
our roundtables with the relevant government agencies listed previously.
Specifically, we relied on a list of experts compiled for the first report
under this mandate. These experts represented a wide range of interests
including academics, industry representatives, judges, and practicing
attorneys. The experts had made proposals, written extensively on
bankruptcies or financial institutions, or were recommended by relevant
government agencies. In addition, relevant government agencies and
NAS suggested additional potential participants for our roundtables,
whom we considered using our original criteria and the balance of the
experts at the roundtables. Final participants for the roundtables were
chosen for their expertise and to ensure that a number of interested
parties were included. These included academics, industry
representatives, judges, practicing attorneys, and regulators. To ensure
that participants represented a broad range of views and interests and
that we fully understood those interests, we required that participants
complete a conflict of interest form. See appendix II for a list of
participants in each roundtable, as well as background materials and
agendas.

Participants at the first roundtable held on April 1, 2013, discussed the
role of regulators in the bankruptcy process for financial companies and
how those bankruptcies might be financed.[3] The proposals discussed
were:

1. Require the debtor to notify and consult with regulators (primary,
   functional, Financial Stability Oversight Council, foreign, or other) in
   advance of filing for bankruptcy.

2. Allow regulators (primary, functional, Financial Stability Oversight
   Council, foreign, or other) to commence an involuntary bankruptcy in
   the event that the firm is insolvent or in imminent danger of becoming
   insolvent.

3. Allow regulators (primary, functional, Financial Stability Oversight
   Council, foreign, or other) of the debtor or its subsidiaries to have
   standing or a right to be heard in the courts to raise issues relative to
   regulation.

---

[3]We provided the experts with another proposal on granting regulators the right to file
reorganization plans and motions for sale of property but experts spent almost no time
addressing it so it is not included in this discussion. See appendix II.

4. Consider the role of regulators (primary, functional, Financial Stability Oversight Council, foreign, or other) in determining what subsidiaries should be included in a bankruptcy proceeding, the extent to which complex firms might be consolidated in bankruptcy, including the possibility of revoking the exclusion from bankruptcy for insurance companies and the exclusion from Chapter 11 for stock and commodities brokers.

5. Restrict U.S. Treasury and Federal Reserve from participating in bankruptcy financing.

6. Allow the government to provide subordinated debtor-in-possession financing to companies with assets greater than $100 million (subsidiaries included) with a hearing and the court's approval and oversight.

Similarly, participants in the second roundtable, held on April 10, 2013, discussed proposals to change the safe-harbor treatment of certain financial contracts such as derivatives and repurchase agreements.[4] The proposals discussed during this roundtable were:

1. Removing all safe harbors for qualified financial contracts.

2. Partially rolling back safe harbors on specific contracts; such as

   a. allowing only contracts traded on an exchange to have safe-harbor treatment;

   b. limiting collateral sales of repos by counterparties to cash-like or highly marketable securities; or

   c. allowing roll backs with approval of the Financial Stability Oversight Council or the courts.

3. Implementing a temporary stay for all or certain contracts.

4. Exercising certain "reach back" avoiding powers for qualified financial contracts.

In both cases participants discussed the advantages and disadvantages of the proposals relative to our criteria for orderly and effective bankruptcies. In addition they discussed impediments to implementing proposals and how these impediments could be addressed. The agendas

---

[4]We provided the experts with another proposal on keeping contracts open after bankruptcy with revaluations determined by the courts, but experts spent almost no time addressing it so it is not included in this discussion. See Appendix II.

for the roundtables are included in appendix II. To meet our objectives,
we also interviewed some experts that were not able or did not choose to
participate in the roundtables on their views about the proposals.

We used regulatory data to provide context for some expert statements.
For expert statements on the growth of large financial institutions since
the 2007-2009 financial crisis, we used data from the Federal Reserve
and SEC to provide measures of the growth of global systemically
important banks from 2007 to 2012. For expert statements about the
growth of markets for repurchase agreements and derivatives related to
changes in the Code in 2005, we used data from FSOC's 2013 Annual
Report, which is signed by the principals of 9 federal agencies and the
independent member with insurance expertise, and the Bank for
International Settlements to provide measures of the growth of
repurchase agreements and derivatives from 2000 to 2012.

We conducted this performance audit from October 2012 to July 2013 in
accordance with generally accepted government auditing standards.
Those standards require that we plan and perform the audit to obtain
sufficient, appropriate evidence to provide a reasonable basis for our
findings and conclusions based on our audit objectives. We believe that
the evidence obtained provides a reasonable basis for our findings and
conclusions based on our audit objectives.

Appendix II: Experts, Background, and Agendas for Expert Roundtables

This appendix includes a list of the experts who participated in our roundtables, background information that was provided to the experts prior to the roundtables, and the agendas for the roundtables discussions.

Expert Participants

Donald Bernstein, Davis Polk & Wardwell
Robert Bliss, Wake Forest University
Patrick Bolton, Columbia University
Josh Cohn, International Swaps and Derivatives Association
Christine M. Cumming, Federal Reserve Bank of New York
Marcia Goldstein, Weil, Gotshal & Manges
Allan Gropper, U.S. Bankruptcy Court, Southern District of New York
Randall Guynn, Davis Polk & Wardwell
Kevin Kelly, JPMorgan Chase & Co.
Michael Krimminger, Cleary Gottlieb Steen & Hamilton
Christopher LaRosa, Securities Investor Protection Corp.
Stephen Lubben, Seton Hall University
Carter McDowell, Securities Industry and Financial Markets Association
Thomas McGowan, Securities and Exchange Commission
Knox McIlwain, Cleary Gottlieb Steen & Hamilton
James Millstein, Millstein & Co.
Edward Morrison, University of Chicago
James Peck, U.S. Bankruptcy Court, Southern District of New York
Mark Roe, Harvard University
Paul Saltzman, The Clearing House
Kenneth Scott, Stanford University
Bruce Tuckman, New York University
David Wall, Federal Deposit Insurance Corp.
Mary Walrath, U.S. Bankruptcy Court, District of Delaware
Robert Wasserman, Commodity Futures Trading Commission

Background Information-Roundtable 1

National Academies/Government Accountability Office Roundtable on
Role of Regulators and the Treasury in Financial Company Bankruptcies
Information for Participants

Introduction

This roundtable will inform potential findings for the U.S. Government Accountability Office's (GAO) ongoing work on the effectiveness of the U.S. Bankruptcy Code (Code) in facilitating the orderly liquidation or reorganization of financial companies. Congress mandated this work under Section 202(e) of the Dodd-Frank Wall Street Reform and Consumer Protection Act. Among other things, GAO's first report in response to this mandate—*Bankruptcy: Complex Financial Institutions and International Coordination Pose Challenges* (GAO-11-707)—developed criteria for orderly and effective bankruptcies and cataloged proposals for revising the Code to improve the orderliness and effectiveness of financial company bankruptcies. This GAO bankruptcy study will focus on the advantages and disadvantages of some proposals to change the Code to make bankruptcies of financial companies—especially those posing systemic risk—more orderly and effective.

Under a standing arrangement between the two institutions, GAO has asked the National Academies to host this meeting and help identify and invite participants. This roundtable provides a forum for experts with different backgrounds and experience to discuss some of the key issues concerning possible bankruptcy reforms, including potential outcomes, consequences, and tradeoffs. GAO identified these issues through literature reviews and interviews with a broad range of experts from the financial regulatory and legal communities, academia, and the financial services industry. An agenda for the meeting with location and time is appended to this document.

Proposals

During the April 1, 2013 Bankruptcy Roundtable, participants will be asked to discuss their views and insights on elements of proposals GAO identified that focus on changing the role of financial regulators in Chapter 11 cases involving financial institutions. Such proposals include

- requiring the debtor to notify and consult with regulators in advance of filing for bankruptcy;

- allowing regulators to commence an involuntary bankruptcy in the event that the firm is insolvent or in imminent danger of becoming insolvent;

- allowing regulators (primary, functional, Financial Stability Oversight Council, foreign, or other) of the debtor or its subsidiaries to have standing or a right to be heard in the courts to raise issues relative to regulation;

- allowing regulators (primary, functional, Financial Stability Oversight Council, foreign, or other) of the debtor or its subsidiaries to file plans for reorganization and motions under Section 363, such as motions for the use, sale, and lease of property; and

- considering the role of regulators in determining what subsidiaries should be included in a bankruptcy proceeding, the extent to which complex firms might be consolidated in bankruptcy, including the possibility of revoking the exclusion from bankruptcy for insurance companies and the exclusion from Chapter 11 for stock and commodities brokers.

Furthermore, proposals have been made to limit or specify the ability of the Treasury or the Federal Reserve to help finance bankruptcies of financial institutions. The roundtable will consider the proposals and discuss the appropriate role of the government in providing financing for firms in bankruptcy. The proposals to be discussed are

National Academies/Government Accountability Office Roundtable on
Role of Regulators and the Treasury in Financial Company Bankruptcies
Information for Participants

- bills introduced in the 111th Congress that specifically would forbid the U.S. Treasury and Federal Reserve from participating in bankruptcy financing; and

- the Chapter 14 proposal made by the Working Group on Economic Policy at the Hoover Institution that would allow the government to provide subordinated debtor-in-possession financing to companies with assets greater than $100 million (subsidiaries included) with a hearing and the court's approval and oversight.

Further details on the proposals listed above may be found in the following sources:

- Robert Bliss and George Kaufman. "Resolving Large Complex Financial Institutions: The Case for Reorganization." April 2011. http://www.clevelandfed.org/research/conferences/2011/4-14-2011/Bliss_kaufman.pdf.

- Kenneth E. Scott and Thomas Jackson, eds., *Bankruptcy Not Bailout: A Special Chapter 14* (Stanford, Calif.: Hoover Institution Press, 2012).

- Institute for International Finance. *Making Resolution Robust: Completing the Legal and Institutional Frameworks for Effective Cross-Border Resolution of Financial Institutions.* (Washington, D.C.: Institute for International Finance, June 2012).

- Consumer Protection and Regulatory Enhancement Act. HR 3310, 111th Cong., 1st sess., *Congressional Record* (July 24, 2009): E1964-E1967.

- *Bankruptcy Integrity and Accountability Act*, Senate Amendment 3832, 111th Cong., 2nd sess., *Congressional Record* (May 5, 2010): S3620-3624.

Criteria for Orderly and Effective Resolutions or Bankruptcies for Financial Institutions

Roundtable participants will be asked to discuss the proposals with consideration of their possible effects on the orderliness and effectiveness of the bankruptcy process. For our July 2011 report *Bankruptcy: Complex Financial Institutions and International Coordination Pose Challenges* (GAO-11-707), we interviewed legal, economic, and finance experts and reviewed relevant literature to develop criteria for orderly and effective bankruptcies of financial companies. We found that orderliness and effectiveness generally were associated with the following characteristics:

- Limit systemic risk
- Avoid asset fire sales
- Preserve due process
  - Ensure predictability and transparency
  - Ensure creditor rights
- Maximize Value
  - Of the firm in a reorganization
  - To the creditors in a liquidation
- Limit taxpayer liability

2

National Academies/Government Accountability Office Roundtable on
Role of Regulators and the Treasury in Financial Company Bankruptcies
Information for Participants

The principles we established for orderly and effective resolutions are generally consistent with those described in the Financial Stability Board's October 2011 report *Key Attributes of Effective Resolution Regimes for Financial Institutions*, and with principles described in our 2009 report on proposals to modernize the U.S. financial regulatory system.

Further details on the criteria described above may be found in the following sources:

- GAO, *Bankruptcy: Complex Financial Institutions and International Coordination Pose Challenges*, GAO-11-707 (Washington, D.C.: July 19, 2011).

- GAO, *Financial Regulation: A Framework for Crafting and Assessing Proposals to Modernize the Outdated U.S. Financial Regulatory System*, GAO-09-216 (Washington, D.C.: July 22, 2009).

- Financial Stability Board, *Key Attributes of Effective Resolution Regimes for Financial Institutions* (Washington, D.C.: October 2011).

Roundtable Sessions and Topics for Discussion

The roundtable will consist of three sessions that have been structured to help GAO examine potential complexities in and effects of implementing proposed reforms. The first session focuses on the practical mechanics of the proposed changes to the Code. The second session focuses on potential outcomes of the proposals and effects on orderliness and effectiveness. The final session focuses on the challenges of financing large financial company bankruptcies.

Session 1: Implications for Regulators and Courts of Proposals for Changing Regulatory Input

Background
GAO is interested in the mechanics of the changes in the role of regulators in the identified proposals and what the "on the ground" implications might be if these changes were enacted. For example, which regulators would a financial company notify of an intent to file a bankruptcy, and how would the regulator(s) be notified.

Topics for Discussion

- Changes from current regulatory and court activities
- Possible regulatory and legal impediments
- Modifications to proposals to overcome impediments

Session 2: Relationship of Potential Outcomes of Proposals to Measures of Orderliness and Effectiveness

Background
Changes to regulatory input in the bankruptcy process may have a range of effects. GAO is interested in how the outcomes of the proposed changes might be evaluated using the criteria of orderliness and effectiveness. Characteristics of orderliness and effectiveness in a financial company bankruptcy include mitigating systemic risk, avoiding asset fire sales, ensuring due

3

National Academies/Government Accountability Office Roundtable on
Role of Regulators and the Treasury in Financial Company Bankruptcies
Information for Participants

process, maximizing value, and minimizing taxpayer cost.

<u>Topics for Discussion</u>

- Likely short-term outcomes
- Potential secondary effects
- Effects on the orderliness and effectiveness of financial company bankruptcies and potential tradeoffs among criteria
- Modifications to proposals to minimize any negative impacts

Session 3: Financing Financial Company Bankruptcies with Minimal Taxpayer Liability

<u>Background</u>

One principle for an effective bankruptcy or resolution process is to limit taxpayer liability, and bills introduced in the 111th Congress specifically forbid the U.S. Treasury and Federal Reserve from participating in bankruptcy financing. However, some proposals recognize the difficulty of financing bankruptcies of large financial companies, especially during a crisis. For example, Chapter 14 would allow the federal government to provide subordinated debtor-in-possession financing to companies with assets greater than $100 million (subsidiaries included) with a hearing and the court's approval and oversight.

<u>Topics for Discussion</u>

- Funding challenges for large or multiple financial company bankruptcies
- Federal funding role in previous bankruptcies
- Ways to finance large or multiple financial company bankruptcies that limit taxpayer liability

4

Background Information-Roundtable 2

National Academies/Government Accountability Office Roundtable on
The Treatment of Derivatives in Financial Company Bankruptcies
Information for Participants

Introduction

This roundtable will inform potential findings for the U.S. Government Accountability Office's
(GAO) ongoing work on the effectiveness of the U.S. Bankruptcy Code (Code) in facilitating the
orderly liquidation or reorganization of financial companies. Congress mandated this work under
Section 202(e) of the Dodd-Frank Wall Street Reform and Consumer Protection Act. Among
other things, GAO's first report in response to this mandate—*Bankruptcy: Complex Financial
Institutions and International Coordination Pose Challenges* (GAO-11-707)—developed criteria
for orderly and effective bankruptcies and cataloged proposals for revising the Code to improve
the orderliness and effectiveness of financial company bankruptcies. This GAO bankruptcy
study will focus on the advantages and disadvantages of some proposals to change the Code to
make bankruptcies of financial companies—especially those posing systemic risk—more orderly
and effective.

Under a standing arrangement between the two institutions, GAO has asked the National
Academies to host this meeting and help identify and invite participants. This roundtable
provides a forum for experts with different backgrounds and experience to discuss some of the
key issues concerning possible bankruptcy reforms: potential outcomes, implementation
challenges and tradeoffs, and actions that could be taken to mitigate impediments or tradeoffs.
GAO identified these issues through literature reviews and interviews with a broad range of
experts from the financial regulatory and legal communities, academia, and the financial
services industry. An agenda for the meeting with location and time is appended to this
document.

Proposals

During the April 10, 2013 Bankruptcy Roundtable, participants will be asked to discuss their
views and insights on elements of proposals GAO identified that focus on changing safe harbor
treatment for derivatives and repurchase (repo) contracts that qualify for such treatment—often
called qualified financial contracts or QFCs—as well as the current treatment of such contracts.
Proposals for change include

- Removing all safe harbors for QFCs;
- Rolling back safe harbors on specific contracts;
    - Allowing only contracts traded on an exchange to have safe-harbor treatment;
    - Limiting collateral sales of repos by counterparties to cash-like or highly;
      marketable securities;
    - Allowing roll backs with approval of the Financial Stability Oversight Council or
      the courts;
- Implementing a temporary stay for all or certain contracts;
- Keeping contracts open after bankruptcy with revaluations determined by the courts; and
- Exercising certain "reach back" avoiding powers for QFCs.

Further details on the proposals listed above may be found in the following sources:

- Kenneth E. Scott and Thomas Jackson, eds., *Bankruptcy Not Bailout: A Special
  Chapter 14* (Stanford, Calif.: Hoover Institution Press, 2012).

National Academies/Government Accountability Office Roundtable on
The Treatment of Derivatives in Financial Company Bankruptcies
Information for Participants

- Stephen J. Lubben, "Repeal the Safe Harbors." *American Bankruptcy Institute Law Review*, vol. 18, 2010. http://ssrn.com/abstract=1497040.

- Robert Bliss and George Kaufman, "Resolving Large Complex Financial Institutions: The Case for Reorganization," April 2011. http://www.clevelandfed.org/research/conferences/2011/4-14-2011/Bliss_kaufman.pdf.

- Bruce Tuckman, "Amending Safe Harbors to Reduce Systemic Risk in OTC Derivatives Markets," Center for Financial Stability, working paper, April 22, 2010. http://www.moodys.com/microsites/crc2011/papers/BruceTuckman.pdf.

- Darrell Duffie and David Skeel, "A Dialogue on the Costs and Benefits of Automatic Stays for Derivatives and Repurchase Agreements," University of Pennsylvania Law School, Institute for Law and Economics, Research Paper 12-2, March 2012. http://ssrn.com/abstract=1982095. Also included in *Bankruptcy Not Bailout: A Special Chapter 14*.

- *Consumer Protection and Regulatory Enhancement Act*. HR 3310, 111th Cong., 1st sess., *Congressional Record* (July 24, 2009): E1964-E1967.

- *Bankruptcy Integrity and Accountability Act*, Senate Amendment 3832, 111th Cong., 2nd sess., *Congressional Record* (May 5, 2010): S3620-3624.

Criteria for Orderly and Effective Resolutions or Bankruptcies for Financial Institutions
Roundtable participants will be asked to discuss the proposals with consideration of their possible effects on the orderliness and effectiveness of the bankruptcy process. For our July 2011 report *Bankruptcy: Complex Financial Institutions and International Coordination Pose Challenges* (GAO-11-707), we interviewed legal, economic, and finance experts and reviewed relevant literature to develop criteria for orderly and effective bankruptcies of financial companies. We found that orderliness and effectiveness generally were associated with the following criteria:

- Limit systemic risk

- Avoid asset fire sales

- Preserve due process
    - Ensure predictability and transparency
    - Ensure creditor rights

- Maximize Value
    - Of the firm in a reorganization
    - To the creditors in a liquidation

- Limit taxpayer liability

The criteria we established for orderly and effective resolutions are generally consistent with those described in the Financial Stability Board's October 2011 report *Key Attributes of Effective Resolution Regimes for Financial Institutions*, and with principles described in our 2009 report on proposals to modernize the U.S. financial regulatory system.

2

National Academies/Government Accountability Office Roundtable on
The Treatment of Derivatives in Financial Company Bankruptcies
Information for Participants

Further details on the criteria described above may be found in the following sources:

- GAO, *Bankruptcy: Complex Financial Institutions and International Coordination Pose Challenges*, GAO-11-707 (Washington, D.C.: July 19, 2011).

- GAO, *Financial Regulation: A Framework for Crafting and Assessing Proposals to Modernize the Outdated U.S. Financial Regulatory System*, GAO-09-216 (Washington, D.C.: July 22, 2009).

- Financial Stability Board, *Key Attributes of Effective Resolution Regimes for Financial Institutions* (Washington, D.C.: October 2011).

Roundtable Sessions and Topics for Discussion

The roundtable consists of three sessions that have been structured to help GAO address the effects of the proposed reforms. The first session focuses on the potential outcomes of the proposed changes to safe harbors and any effects on the orderliness and effectiveness of the bankruptcy process. The second session focuses on the potential challenges of implementing the proposed changes and the roles of interested parties. The final session focuses on further actions that might be taken to preserve current treatment benefits or overcome potential challenges for proposals.

Session 1: Potential Outcomes of Proposals

Background

GAO is interested in the outcomes and effects of the proposed changes to safe harbors for QFCs and how such changes might affect the orderliness and effectiveness of the bankruptcy process for financial companies.

Questions for Discussion

- Likely immediate and short-term impact

- Secondary effects (e.g., financial institutions rewriting financial contracts so that they still get safe-harbor treatment)

- Evaluation of current treatment of QFCs and proposals using criteria of orderliness and effectiveness

- Potential tradeoffs among criteria

Session 2: Implementing Change

Background

Changes to safe harbors would affect a number of interested parties. GAO is interested in how the proposed changes might affect the roles of such parties and what the most notable challenges in implementing those changes would be, including the likelihood that experts will agree on the need for specific changes.

3

National Academies/Government Accountability Office Roundtable on
The Treatment of Derivatives in Financial Company Bankruptcies
Information for Participants

Questions for Discussion

- Roles of Congress, courts, and regulators
- Effects on QFC market and market participants
- Challenges to implementing change
- Likelihood of consensus

Session 3: Further Actions

Background

The first two sessions explored possible positive and negative effects of QFC proposals and impediments to implementing those proposals. In this session, GAO is interested in exploring further actions that might be taken to preserve benefits of the current treatment, limit any potential negative effects of the proposals, and overcome any impediments to implementing those proposals. These actions include specific next steps, such as additional studies that need to be performed, or a potential timetable for implementing possible changes in the safe-harbor treatment of QFCs.

Questions for Discussion

- Mitigating any negative effects of proposals while preserving positive aspects of QFC treatment
- Overcoming implementation challenges
- Next steps

4

Roundtable Agendas

Roundtable on Bankruptcy Reform:
Proposed Changes to the Role of Regulators and Treasury in
Financial Company Bankruptcies

Sponsored by the U.S. Government Accountability Office
and Convened by the National Academies
Keck Center – Room 105
500 Fifth Street, NW
Washington, DC, 20001

April 1, 2013

9:30 a.m.	Check-in/Reception
10:00 a.m.	Welcome and Overview of GAO Studies and Roundtable Goals
	Introduction of Panelists and Overview of Meeting Format and Procedures
10:15 a.m.	Discussion Session 1: Implications for Regulators and Courts of Proposals for Changing Regulatory Input
11:45 a.m.	Lunch
12:30 p.m.	Discussion Session 2: Relationship of Potential Outcomes of Such Proposals to Measures of Orderliness and Effectiveness
2:00 p.m.	Break
2:15 p.m.	Discussion Session 3: Financing Financial Company Bankruptcies with Minimal Taxpayer Liability
3:15 p.m.	Wrap-up
4:00 p.m.	Adjourn

Roundtable on Bankruptcy Reform:
Proposed Changes to the Treatment of Derivative Contracts
in Financial Company Bankruptcies

Sponsored by the U.S. Government Accountability Office
and Convened by the National Academies
500 Fifth Street, NW,
Washington, DC, 20001

April 10, 2013

9:30 a.m.	Check-in/Reception
10:00 a.m.	Welcome and Overview of GAO Studies and Roundtable Goals
	Introduction of Panelists and Overview of Meeting Format and Procedures
10:05 a.m.	Discussion Session 1: Potential Outcomes of Proposals
11:00 a.m.	Break
11:10 a.m.	Resume Session 1
12:00 p.m.	Lunch
12:45 p.m.	Discussion Session 2: Implementing Change
2:15 p.m.	Break
2:30 p.m.	Discussion Session 3: Further Actions
3:45 p.m.	Wrap-up
4:00 p.m.	Adjourn

2

Appendix III: Safe-Harbor Treatment of Certain Financial Contracts under the Bankruptcy Code

Overview of Financial Derivatives

Financial derivatives derive their value from an underlying reference item or items, such as equities, debt, exchange rates, and interest rates. Parties involved in financial derivative transactions do not need to own or invest in the underlying reference items, and often do not. These products are agreements that shift risks from one party to another—each commonly referred to as a counterparty. Such shifting of risks may allow companies to offset other risks—hedging—or to take advantage of expectations of obtaining an economic gain due to changes in the value of the underlying reference items—speculation. Although some transactions are bilateral in that they involve only two counterparties, derivatives can be used to structure more complicated arrangements involving multiple transactions and parties.

Financial derivatives are sold and traded on regulated exchanges or in private, over-the-counter markets that allow highly customized transactions specific to the needs of the counterparties. A master netting agreement sets out the terms governing contractual actions between counterparties with multiple derivative contracts. This agreement provides for the net settlement of all contracts, as well as cash collateral, through a single payment, in a single currency, in the event of default on or termination of any one contract. Generally counterparties net payments to each other under the contract, and, if a counterparty defaults, the nondefaulting counterparty can immediately close-out open contracts by netting one against the other. It can also receive payment under what is called set off, which is the discharge of reciprocal or mutual obligations to the extent of the smaller obligation. For example, a nondefaulting bank can take funds from a defaulting party's bank deposit held by the bank as payment for what the bank is owed on a contract it has with the defaulting party as long as the deposit existed prior to the default.

Contracts Qualified for Special Treatment under the Code

Financial derivatives receive special treatment under the Code and thus are sometimes called qualified financial contracts (QFC).[1] The Code includes five categories commonly considered QFCs, which include various types of derivatives. Contracts may fall into more than one category. The Code includes specific definitions of the agreements and transactions covered. In addition, to have protection under the Code, the counterparty with the debtor also must meet specified definitions. The

---

[1] The Code does not define a QFC or use this term specifically.

types of derivatives qualifying for special treatment are generally described as follows:

> **Securities contract.** Securities contact is a broad term defining a financial agreement between counterparties and may include contracts for the purchase and sale of various financial products such as a group or index of securities, mortgage loans, certificates of deposit, and extensions of credit for settlement purposes.[2] Margin loans are one type of extension of credit through a financial intermediary for the purchase, sale, carrying, or trading of securities. Margin loans do not include other loans secured with securities collateral.[3] Securities contracts also include options to purchase and sell securities, or other financial products. Options give their holders the right, but not the obligation, to buy (call option) or sell (put option) a specified amount of the underlying reference item at a predetermined price (strike price) at or before the end of the contract.

> **Commodities contract.** In a commodities contract the commodities buyer agrees to purchase from the commodities seller a fixed quantity of a commodity at a fixed price on a fixed date in the future.[4] Commodities can consist of agricultural goods, metals, and goods used for the production of energy such as crude oil. For example, to hedge against the risk of rising oil prices, oil refineries can enter a commodities contract to fix a price today for a future supply shipment.

> **Forward contract.** A "forward contract" is a contract for the purchase, sale, or transfer of a commodity with a maturity date

---

[2]See 11 U.S.C. § 741(7).

[3]H.R. Rep. No. 109-031.

[4]See 11 U.S.C. § 761(4). Commodity is defined by cross-referencing the Commodity Exchange Act, which defines commodity to include agricultural products and "all services, rights, and interests in which contacts for future delivery are presently or in the future dealt in." A "commodity contract" includes purchases and sales of commodities for future delivery on, or subject to the rules of a contract market or board of trade. *Olympic Natural Gas*, 294 F. 3d 737.741 (5th Cir. 2002).

more than 2 days after the contract is entered into.[5] Under the Code, a forward contract can include, but is not limited to, a lease, swap, hedge transaction, deposit, or loan.[6] As an example, a firm may want to limit risk to fluctuations in service costs, such as electricity prices. The firm may enter into a forward contract with an electricity provider to obtain future service at a fixed rate.

Swap Agreement. A swap involves an ongoing exchange of one or more assets, liabilities, or payments for a specified period. Swaps include interest rate swaps, commodity-based swaps, and broad-based credit default swaps. Security-based swaps include single-name and narrow-based credit default swaps and equity-based swaps.[7] As an example, interest rate swaps allow one party to exchange a stream of variable-rate interest payments for a stream of fixed-rate interest payments. These products help market participants hedge their risks or stabilize their cash flows. Alternatively, market participants may use these products to benefit from an expected change in interest rates. A credit default swap is generally a contract between two parties where the first party promises to pay the second party if a third party experiences a credit event such as failing to pay a debt. Credit default swaps are contracts that act as a type of insurance, or a way to hedge risks, against default or another type of credit event associated with a security such as a corporate bond.

Repurchase agreements are also qualified to receive special treatment under the Code and are thus considered to be a QFC. In a repurchase agreement one party sells a security, or a portfolio of securities, to another party and agrees to repurchase the security or portfolio on a specified future date—often the next day—at a prearranged price.[8] The

---

[5]See 11 U.S.C. § 101(25). The definition of "forward contact" in the Code has been found to include four elements: (1) a contract for the sale of a commodity; (2) with a delivery date more than two days after execution; (3) by a forward contract merchant; and (4) that is not otherwise subject to the rules of a board of trade. See *In re MBS Management Services, Inc.*, 432 B.R. 570 (Bankr. E.D. La. 2010), aff'd 2010 WL 1899764 (E.D. La. 2011).

[6]Outside of the Code, a forward contract has been referred to as a contract whereby the forward buyer agrees to purchase from the forward seller a fixed quantity of the underlying reference item at a fixed price on a fixed date in the future.

[7]See 11 U.S.C. § 101(53B).

[8]See 11 U.S.C. § 101(47).

security, or portfolio of securities, serves as collateral for the transaction. In a reverse repurchase agreement, a security is purchased with the agreement to resell on a specified future date. Repurchase agreements have been used to provide financial institutions with funding for operations.

A bilateral repurchase agreement—a repurchase agreement solely between two counterparties—can be viewed as two subtransactions referred to as initiation and completion.[9] A repurchase agreement is similar to a loan secured by collateral. A firm will lend cash to a counterparty at an interest rate in exchange for assets provided by the counterparty as collateral. In a repurchase agreement, a cash provider willing to invest cash will agree to purchase securities from a collateral provider, or repurchase agreement dealer. Repurchase agreement dealers are typically distinguished as the counterparty selling securities, or providing collateral, at initiation. The market value of the securities purchased will typically exceed the value of cash loaned to the dealer. When a repurchase agreement matures, securities are sold back to the collateral provider and cash plus interest are returned to the cash provider. Collateral providers or dealers are generally large financial institutions, such as subsidiaries within bank holding companies. Cash providers are firms such as, but not limited to, other large financial institutions, hedge funds, and money market funds. Under the Code, U.S. Treasury debt securities, agency debt issues, mortgage-backed securities, and other assets can be used as collateral in repurchase agreement transactions.

Treatment of QFCs under the Code

For most of the debtor's assets, the Code provides an automatic stay, or freeze, when the bankruptcy petition is filed. That is, the filing generally stops lawsuits, foreclosures, and most other collection activities against the debtor allowing the debtor or a trustee time to eliminate or restructure debts. For example, set-off of any debt owed to the debtor that arose before the filing against any claim against the debtor is prohibited.[10] Additionally, in certain situations debtors may not terminate or modify an

---

[9]Triparty repurchase agreements include three parties: the borrower, the lender, and a triparty agent that facilitates the repurchase agreement transaction by providing custody of the securities posted as collateral and valuing the collateral, among other services.

[10]11 U.S.C. § 362(a).

executory contract at any time after the bankruptcy is filed solely because of a provision in the contract that is conditioned on the insolvency or financial condition of the debtor or the filing of bankruptcy or the appointing of a trustee.[11] However, the QFC's described previously receive safe-harbor treatment that generally exempts them from the automatic stay. Instead, the contractual rights—to liquidate, accelerate, or terminate—of nondefaulting counterparties conditioned on the insolvency or financial condition of one of the counterparties or the filing of bankruptcy or the appointing of a trustee, such as netting and setoff, are activated.[12] Counterparties with claims against the debtor's property are typically referred to as creditors.

Some contracts that are generally considered QFCs may not be eligible for safe-harbor treatment or may be otherwise limited. For example:

- Repurchase agreements, where the debtor is a stockbroker or securities clearing agency, and securities contracts that are resolved under the Securities Investor Protection Act of 1970 (SIPA) or any statute administered by Securities and Exchange Commission (SEC).[13]

- Certain commodity contracts involved in a commodity broker's liquidation under Chapter 7. For example, a commodity broker creditor may not net or offset an obligation to a commodity broker debtor.[14]

- Repurchase agreements are treated differently from some other contracts in that any excess of the market prices received on liquidation over the amount of the stated repurchase agreement price and all expenses in connection with the liquidation of the repurchase

---

[11]11 U.S.C. § 365(e)(1). In bankruptcy, an executory contract is one in which both parties to the contract have future performance obligations that, if unperformed by either party, would result in a material breach. See Regen Capital I, Inc., v. Halperin, 547 F. 3d 484 (2d Cir. 2008); Olah v. Baird, 567 F. 3d 1207 (10th Cir. 2009).

[12]See 11 U.S.C. §§ 555, 556, 559, 560. Note that the phrase "liquidate, terminate and accelerate" was added to the Code through amendments in 2005. Previously, the right to liquidate was provided for securities contracts, commodity contracts, forward contracts and repurchase agreements, while the right to terminate was provided for swaps. H.R. Rep. No. 109-031.

[13]11 U.S.C. § 555; 11 U.S.C. § 559.

[14]11 U.S.C. § 561(b)(2).

agreement must be deemed property of the debtor's estate, subject to the available rights of setoff.[15]

- For master netting agreements, the right to terminate, liquidate, or accelerate is only applicable to the extent it is permissible for each type of QFC.[16]

After entities exercise their rights of netting for individual QFCs and under master netting agreements, some debtors still may be indebted to the creditor. Generally, the creditors' remaining claims will receive the same treatment accorded other unsecured creditors.[17]

The figures below illustrate the safe-harbor exemption from the automatic stay in simplified, yet practical scenarios:

Figure 4 illustrates a bilateral contract, in which two counterparties are able to net opposing obligations of a contract, or, stated otherwise, net payments under a single master netting agreement. In this example, under current market conditions of an existing QFC, Firm A owes $100 to Firm B while Firm B owes $120 to Firm A. If Firm B files under the Code, the QFC is not stayed due to the safe harbor and Firm A receives the net proceeds of $20 ahead of Firm B's other creditors. However, Firm A has no guarantee of recouping the total value from the QFC due to other factors, such as a change in market conditions. Without the safe harbors, Firm A would not have been able to terminate the transaction and could have been exposed to further market risk.

---

[15]11 U.S.C. § 559.

[16]11 U.S.C. § 561(a).

[17]See 11 U.S.C. § 753; 11 U.S.C. § 767.

Figure 4: QFC Termination and the Netting of Obligations

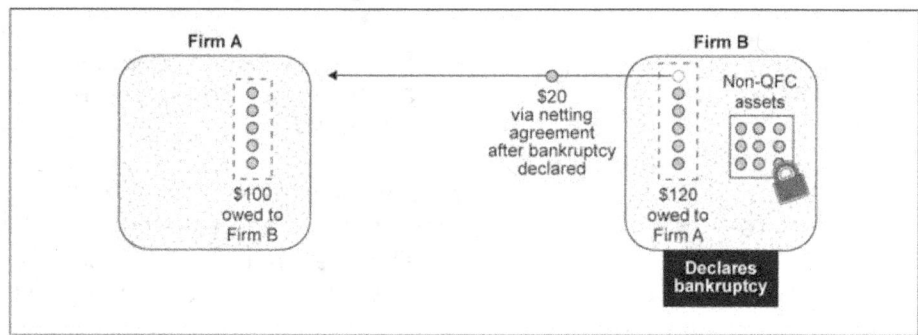

Qualified financial contract (QFC)

Source: GAO.

Figure 5 depicts the typical completion of a repurchase agreement transaction along with the possibility that the creditor liquidates collateral in certain situations. In the case of a repurchase agreement, if a dealer files under the Code after the initiation but prior to completion, the cash provider at initiation will be left with the collateral provided by the dealer. Under the safe harbor, the cash provider has the option to terminate the transaction with the insolvent dealer. As illustrated in figure 4, the cash provider may terminate the transaction and sell the collateral in the open market to a third party. Without the safe harbor, concerns have been raised that a stay on the overnight repurchase agreement market could result in adverse market impacts due to simultaneous sales of collateral.

Figure 5: Completion of Bilateral Repurchase Agreement and Collateral Liquidation

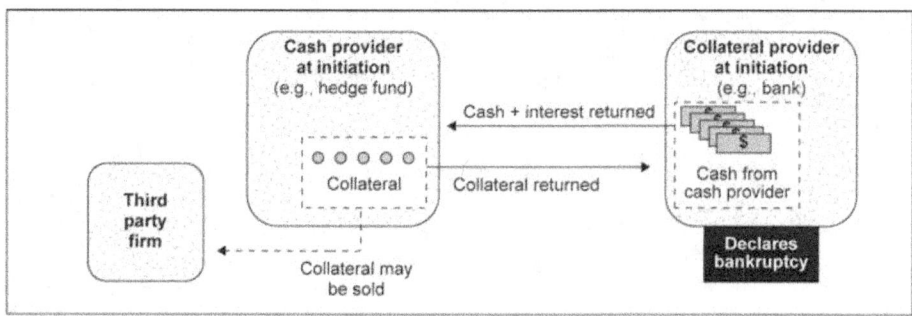

Bilateral repurchase agreement as qualified financial contract (QFC)

Source: GAO.

QFCs are generally also exempt from avoidance or claw back provisions under the Code. These provisions generally require that the trustee may avoid, or take back, any payments made during the 90 days before the filing of a bankruptcy petition if those payments are preferential or 2 years before the filing of the petition if those payments are fraudulent.[18] But, for QFCs, a trustee may not recover certain transfers made by or to a swap participant, repurchase agreement participant, commodity broker, forward contract merchant, stockbroker, financial institution, financial participant, or securities clearing agency in connection with securities contracts, commodity contracts, forward contracts, repurchase agreements, or swaps that were done before the bankruptcy filing.[19] Also, a trustee may not recover transfers made by or to a master netting agreement participant or any individual contract covered by a master netting agreement that was made before the bankruptcy filing.[20] Since many QFCs are short term, and likely to be agreed to well within the 90 day window, these exemptions provide protection to many QFCs including those under master netting agreements.

---

[18] 11 U.S.C. § 547; 11 U.S.C. § 548.

[19] 11 U.S.C. § 546(e), (f) and (g).

[20] 11 U.S.C. § 546(j). For both 11 U.S.C. § 546(e), (f), (g) and (j), the protection from pull back is not provided if the transfer was done based on fraud under 11 U.S.C. § 548(a)(1). For the master netting agreements it cannot be more than the extent that the trustee could otherwise avoid the transfer made under an individual contract covered by the master netting agreement. 11 U.S.C. § 546(j).

DEPARTMENT OF THE TREASURY
WASHINGTON, D.C

UNDER SECRETARY

July 10, 2013

Ms. Alicia Puente Cackley
Director, Financial Markets and Community Investment
Government Accountability Office
441 G St., NW
Washington, D.C. 20548

Dear Ms. Puente Cackley:

I am writing on behalf of Secretary Lew, who is the Chairperson of the Financial Stability
Oversight Council (Council). We appreciate the opportunity to review the Government
Accountability Office's (GAO) draft report GAO-13-622 (the Draft Report) regarding
advantages and disadvantages of certain proposals to revise the Bankruptcy Code for financial
company bankruptcies.

The Council shares the GAO's concern that a disorderly financial company bankruptcy could
pose risks to financial stability. However, the Dodd-Frank Wall Street Reform and Consumer
Protection Act (the Act) provided regulators with important new tools to address these concerns,
and until such tools are fully implemented or there is evidence of risks that cannot be adequately
addressed within existing law, it would be premature for the Council to prioritize the
consideration of proposals to amend the Bankruptcy Code. Importantly, the Board of Governors
of the Federal Reserve System (Federal Reserve Board) and the Federal Deposit Insurance
Corporation are currently implementing provisions of the Act requiring financial companies to
submit resolution plans ("living wills") to facilitate their orderly resolution under the Bankruptcy
Code in the event of their material financial distress or failure. These living wills are a critical
element of the bankruptcy process for large financial companies. It is important to allow the
regulators sufficient time to evaluate these plans, especially given that not all covered companies
have made their first submissions.

The Council is focused on efforts that most effectively achieve its statutory mandate to respond
to emerging threats to the stability of the U.S. financial system. The Council is engaged in a
wide variety of actions to address risks to financial stability posed by the failure of one or more
financial companies, including:

- Designating nonbank financial companies whose material financial distress could pose a
  threat to financial stability for supervision by the Federal Reserve Board. The
  designation of these nonbank financial companies also subjects these firms to enhanced
  prudential standards which will reduce the likelihood, and the severity of the impact on
  U.S. financial stability, of their failure.

- Facilitating communication and coordination on the implementation of the orderly liquidation authority, resolution plans, and other aspects of existing law that seek to mitigate risks to financial stability from the disorderly failure of a financial company.

- Engaging in real-time monitoring and communication about risks to financial stability, such as risks posed by Superstorm Sandy and the bankruptcy filing of MF Global. As the Draft Report notes, the Council met in emergency session on the day MF Global declared bankruptcy to monitor the event and its impact on markets.

The Draft Report recommends that the Council consider proposals from the 111th Congress as well as proposals from certain academic and research-focused sources. These proposals included changing the role of financial regulators in the bankruptcy process and the treatment of qualified financial contracts. The GAO held two expert roundtables in which participants evaluated these proposals. While the Council recognizes that discussing and making recommendations to Congress on various possible changes to the Bankruptcy Code could contribute to the debate on these issues, the Draft Report notes that GAO's panel of experts was not ready to recommend specific changes to the Bankruptcy Code—a further indication that Council prioritization of these proposals would be premature.

We strongly support GAO's efforts to carry out its responsibilities under the Act. Although we have concerns with the Draft Report's recommendation, we are committed to the implementation of the Act and continuing our efforts to fulfill the statutory mission of the Council in the most effective, efficient, and transparent way possible. Thank you again for the opportunity to engage with your staff over the past three years in fulfilling your mandate to study this issue and to review and comment on the Draft Report. We look forward to working with you in the future.

Sincerely,

Mary J. Miller

Appendix V: GAO Contact and Staff Acknowledgments

GAO Contact	Alicia Puente Cackley, (202) 512-8678 or cackleya@gao.gov
Staff Acknowledgments	In addition to the contact named above, Debra Johnson (Assistant Director), Nancy S. Barry, Rudy Chatlos, Risto Laboski, Marc Molino, Barbara Roesmann, Jessica Sandler, and Jason Wildhagen made significant contributions to this report. Other assistance was provided by Janet Eackloff and Walter Vance.